NABC's Handbook for Teaching
Basketball Skill Progressions

Specifically Designed for Players Ages 4 to 18

Jerry Krause, Gonzaga University

Curtis Janz, Oklahoma Christian University

James Conn, Central Missouri State University

COACHES CHOICE™

ISBN: 978-1-58518-857-4
Library of Congress Control Number: 2003103856

Book layout and cover design: Jennifer Bokelmann
Text photos: Chelsea Fine, Gonzaga University Sports Information Department
Front cover photo: David Taylor/Allsport

Coaches Choice
P.O. Box 1828
Monterey, CA 93942
www.coacheschoice.com

ACKNOWLEDGMENTS

My gratitude goes to my loving sister, Crystal, who has been the editing/word processing beacon for all of my books. I will always use her standards of excellence as a guide. Thanks to my coauthors, Curtis Janz, who provided the idea for this book, Jim Conn, my long time friend who shares my love of basketball, and Dan Hays, who inspired me to teach and examine the fundamental skills. Appreciation also goes to Gonzaga University—our basketball coaches and administrators who have provided the setting for growing this legacy. Matt and Debbie Sevareid have compiled this publication and provided the glue to hold it together. Chelsea Fine of the Zag Sports Information Office was the photographer for the many illustrations that clarify the skills so necessary to master the sport. Finally, Jim Peterson of Coaches Choice has always supported my basketball efforts – for this I am extremely thankful.

— Jerry Krause

Many of the concepts in this book I have learned from the outstanding coaches I have worked with at Oklahoma Christian Cage Camps or on the staff at Oklahoma Christian University. I would like to thank some of those people: Ralph Nigro, Edmond North High School (OK); Robert Foreman, Westmoore High School (OK); Ralph Turner, Union University; Bob Hoffman, UT Pan American; Steve Dodd, Russell High School (KY); Tony Robinson, Southeastern State University (OK); Scott Morris, Northern Oklahoma College, Enid; and Sherri Coale,University of Oklahoma. Special thanks goes to Jerry Krause, who helped make a good idea a reality, and to Dan Hays (Oklahoma Christian University), my mentor, teacher, and friend. Also, to my father, Lewie Janz, who taught me to love the game. Finally, to my wife, Kathryn, for her continuing support and love.

— Curtis Janz

I have enjoyed the opportunity to participate in such a worthwhile project with my mentor, Dr. Jerry Krause, and Curtis Janz. Recognition goes to my elementary, junior high, and high school coaches, Mr. Clarence Campbell, Mr. Robert Conn, Mr. Moe Rhody, Mr. Berlin Rowe, and Mr. Max Eby, who taught me the fundamentals of basketball and a deep appreciation for the activity. I thank college coaches Mr. Rudy Gerstner and Dr. George H. Sage for helping me shape my coaching philosophy. I also appreciate the opportunities that Dr. Jerry Krause and Mr. Thurman Wright gave me to coach at the university level notwithstanding the experiences I had at South Kitsap High School and Ocosta High School. The game of basketball has been a primary focus of my entire preadolescent and adult life. A special thanks to Dr. Jerry Krause, my mentor, who has always been available for me as a professional and a personal friend since 1967. And a final note of thanks goes to my wife, Linda, who patiently allowed me to fulfill my dreams of coaching basketball and to my children, Allyson, Heather, Jacqueline, and Aaron who endured the games.

— Jim Conn

PREFACE

The idea for this book came from Coach Curtis Janz of Oklahoma Christian University. Curtis is a major part of one of the country's most successful basketball summer camps where over 3,000 campers make their annual trek to Oklahoma City to participate. What is so unique about these camps is their total focus on teaching, learning, and acquiring the fundamental skills needed to play the great game of basketball. Out of this great environment came the question of what to teach and at what age level (i.e., when) to teach these skills.

Dan Hays, a colleague and the head men's basketball coach at Oklahoma Christian University, and I have wrestled with this question since the early 1970s when we coached together. With this common interest, it was decided to develop a guidebook for coaches to answer that question. The purpose of our quest has been to develop a book of guidelines for what is termed "developmentally appropriate" skills for basketball for grade levels K–12 (ages 4–18). This book responds to the questions of what skills should be taught and when is the best age to teach them. This seems even more important today where many coaches of younger players are not trained educators. They may know basketball, but they don't necessarily know how to teach (and develop) players to play the game of basketball.

We have developed a master list of all fundamental skill areas; we have also described those skills and listed critical coaching cues that are necessary teaching points for each skill. Then, the developmentally appropriate skills for the primary grade groupings (K–3, 4–6, 7–8, 9–10, 11–12) are identified. Finally, the skills at each grade level have been placed on a master flow chart for coaches to view the big picture of skill development. Further youth sport resources are also listed.

Jim Conn, a motor learning development expert and former basketball coach with experience from elementary through college levels, has been our final check for "teaching the right skills at the right time."

We believe this guidebook will be valuable for coaches at all grade levels (K–12) and ages (4–18) to:

- focus on the correct skills taught at the appropriate time
- check the present plan of skill teaching
- provide a comprehensive guide for basketball skill teaching (K–12)
- verify the content and timing of the approach to fundamentals
- apply motor development/motor learning concepts to basketball
- fill the need for such a guidebook identified by many coaches we have talked with and observed

It is our hope that you will benefit from and enjoy this basketball guidebook—it is one resource I have long desired to have in print throughout my half-century involvement in the game.

— Jerry Krause
Gonzaga University

DIAGRAM LEGEND

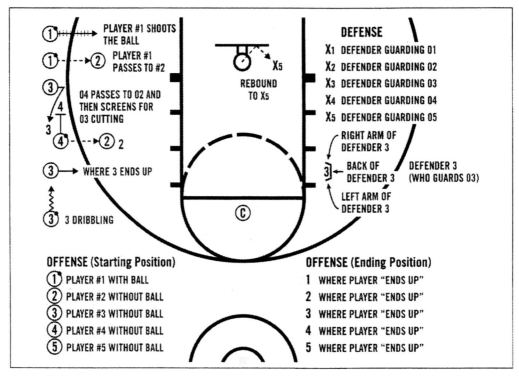

PLAYER #1 SHOOTS THE BALL

PLAYER #1 PASSES TO #2

04 PASSES TO 02 AND THEN SCREENS FOR 03 CUTTING

WHERE 3 ENDS UP

3 DRIBBLING

REBOUND TO X5

DEFENSE

X1 DEFENDER GUARDING 01
X2 DEFENDER GUARDING 02
X3 DEFENDER GUARDING 03
X4 DEFENDER GUARDING 04
X5 DEFENDER GUARDING 05

RIGHT ARM OF DEFENDER 3

BACK OF DEFENDER 3

DEFENDER 3 (WHO GUARDS 03)

LEFT ARM OF DEFENDER 3

OFFENSE (Starting Position)

1 PLAYER #1 WITH BALL
2 PLAYER #2 WITHOUT BALL
3 PLAYER #3 WITHOUT BALL
4 PLAYER #4 WITHOUT BALL
5 PLAYER #5 WITHOUT BALL

OFFENSE (Ending Position)

1 WHERE PLAYER "ENDS UP"
2 WHERE PLAYER "ENDS UP"
3 WHERE PLAYER "ENDS UP"
4 WHERE PLAYER "ENDS UP"
5 WHERE PLAYER "ENDS UP"

Note: All fundamentals are important for all players regardless of size and position. In elementary grades all players should play all positions. It is important that all players are taught all fundamentals. Concentrate on fundamentals more than positions.

CONTENTS

CHAPTER 1

Developing a Coaching Philosophy for Youth Sports

"Focus on fun and fundamentals."

— The Authors

Many former basketball players and coaches grew up in a time when sports were informal, recreational, and controlled by kids. Some people feel that developing a love for the game or being turned on to a sport is enhanced by informal play that is organized by the players. In other words, learning to love basketball as a worthwhile activity is best accomplished when young people organize, coach, officiate, and play the sport by themselves.

This is a far cry from how most kids learn to play basketball—organized leagues, overzealous (and sometimes misinformed and untrained) coaches, over-involved parents, ambitious officials and an overemphasis on competition and winning. That is not a pretty picture of youth basketball.

Thus, a need was identified for a basketball guide for coaches and parents of younger players. Answers to the questions of *what* skills should be taught and *when* they should be taught are provided in this guide. In addition, other related topics are also developed: the appropriate philosophy for youth basketball; organizing and planning practice/play sessions; and making the necessary, age-appropriate modifications for optimal learning. Finally, a sequential, progressive approach to youth basketball that is developmentally appropriate for all age levels is developed and presented.

As we examine the status of sports in the twenty-first century, we note a real dichotomy. On the one hand, we have what is called "business/entertainment sports" contrasted with what we will term "educational sports."

The concept of educational sports focuses on the *development* of the athlete or, more correctly, the development of the whole person who is playing the sport. In this framework, basketball is a medium for educating the person (i.e., sport education) as a means to that end. Most sports decisions in educational sports are made with the player's welfare foremost. For example, players could be encouraged to "call their own fouls" (i.e., self-officiate) in order to accept responsibility to develop the habit of "doing the right thing." Peer pressure is then allowed to influence the development of honesty. Basketball in this format is more focused on education and development of the physical (skills and condition), emotional, and social aspects of the game. Playing for fun and the love of the game is the primary focus.

At the other end of the sports continuum is the "pay for play" emphasis(i.e., business/entertainment sports). In this format, winning is paramount and success is most often defined in terms of winning and/or money. This is exemplified by professional sports and to some extent college and high school sports.

Certainly, sports are hardly ever strictly educational or business, but they operate somewhere along the sports continuum shown in Figure 1.1.

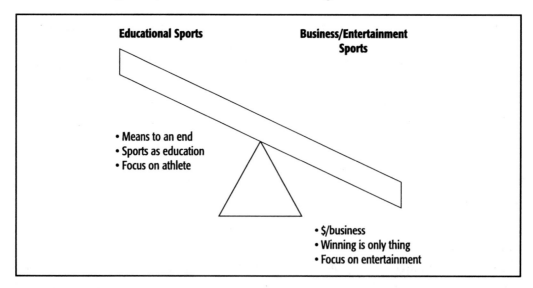

Figure 1.1 — The Sports Continuum

As we focus on youth basketball from preschool to K–12 school sports, it is important to consider what would be the best experience for young people in those basketball settings. It is *strongly* recommended that the philosophy of basketball be geared toward the educational sports end of the continuum. We could characterize this with the philosophical foundation of 'athletes first, winning second,' as advocated by the American Sport Education Program (ASEP).

According to a *USA Today* survey of youth sports participants, more than 75 percent of kids who started playing at age six or seven have quit by the age of 15. The primary reason listed was because it's not fun anymore. Therefore, the primary focus of youth basketball should be rooted in teaching the fundamentals of the game and making it fun as well.

Fun and Fundamentals

It is noteworthy to apply the ASEP philosophy of 'athletes first, winning second' by concentrating on developing kids through basketball where it is perceived as fun. This approach consists of teaching the fundamental basketball skills: footwork (stance and steps); ball handling (dribbling, passing, and catching); shooting; rebounding; and individual defense. Children perceive this experience as hard work, but mastering these skills can lead to delight—a sense of accomplishment through achieving worthwhile skill goals and, eventually, fun and self-confidence derived from worthwhile challenges.

It is also important to develop a definition of success that is achievable by each player and is not necessarily related to winning. The best definition from the basketball world is that of John Wooden, the legendary former UCLA coach. His definition allows each child the chance to succeed and have fun through that achievement. Wooden states, "Success is peace of mind that is a direct result of self-satisfaction in knowing you did your best to become the best you are capable of becoming." Success in youth basketball should be centered around individuals doing their best.

CHAPTER 2

Changing the Game for Younger Players

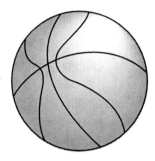

"Success is peace of mind that is a direct result of self-satisfaction in knowing you did your best to become the best you are capable of becoming."

— John Wooden, Naismith Basketball Hall of Fame coach

Basketball is only a game—a sport used to teach children and youth the lessons of sport and life. However, these same youngsters view basketball as the number one team sport in the United States. Thus, those who are involved in sport supervision have a responsibility to not only structure the sport so each participant can become successful, but also to design the experience so it is developmentally appropriate for all players. Let's first examine the origins of basketball to give an understanding and perspective of how this popular sport was invented in America and then developed into a global sport.

Basketball was invented in 1891 by Canadian James Naismith at Springfield College (MA) where he was a graduate assistant. He was assigned the task of developing an indoor game to keep the "YMCA Secretaries" who were being trained there busy and out of trouble during the winter months.

His "peach basket" sport was envisioned as a recreational activity and he was astounded to see basketball-trained YMCA managers spread the game around the world. Naismith lived to see it adopted as an Olympic sport in 1936.

Today, this American sport has spread around the world and is played in over 300 countries. It is a game that can be played in modified form at almost all age levels, starting at around 4-years old, as well as all skill levels, from players with disabilities to elite athletes. Both genders have also popularized the game as a participation sport and a spectator sport.

In the United States, basketball interest is at an all-time high as a spectator sport. However, some educators caution that it is becoming a hollow sport focused on the professional sports model (i.e., a business or entertainment with winning as its sole focus), rather than being built on the solid foundation of broad-based participation. This trend is compounded by today's media age where young and old alike form their notions of basketball from television images of professional and big time basketball where play is often directed toward style more than substance.

As described in Chapter 1, youth basketball should be centered upon the educational sports model (i.e., player centered, participation oriented, developmentally focused). This model could counter the hollow sport trend toward a spectator emphasis and the high dropout rate from biddy basketball to the high school level. It is generally recognized that administrators, officials, and coaches (sport educators) of youth basketball must provide leadership concerning proper philosophy and guidelines for youth sports. Children or society in general can't be expected to provide direction for programs. Thus, the byword for administrators and coaches should be: set the standard, and maintain the standard for educational basketball.

In 1990, the Athletic Footwear Association (AFA), in conjunction with the Youth Sports Institute at Michigan State University, published a comprehensive study— *American Youth and Sports Participation*. Their findings illustrate the importance of factors such as enjoyment in sports, skill development, self-knowledge, and intrinsic rewards for youth sports programs. Similar results have been found in studies done this millennium.

It is important for sport administrators to remind themselves of the reason children play sports *and* stop playing sports. This motive is seen in the following study summary.

The AFA study also depicts in Figure 2.2 the delicate balance that administrators must attain to provide sport experiences that are appropriate for all children. Skill development needs to be balanced with challenges to maximize the chance for enjoyment (defined as fun or success in meeting sport challenges).

This philosophical framework for youth sport standards should also include the ASEP philosophy *Bill of Rights for Young Athletes* that was developed by the National Association for Sport and Physical Education (NASPE).

THE 10 MOST IMPORTANT REASONS I PLAY MY BEST SCHOOL SPORT	**THE 11 MOST IMPORTANT REASONS I STOPPED PLAYING A SPORT**
1. To have fun	1. I lost interest
2. To improve my skills	2. I was not having fun
3. To stay in shape	3. It took too much time
4. To do something I'm good at	4. Coach was a poor teacher
5. For the excitement of competition	5. Too much pressure (worry)
6. To get exercise	6. Wanted non-sport activity
7. To play as part of a team	7. I was tired of it
8. For the challenge of competition	8. Needed more study time
9. To learn new skills	9. Coach played favorites
10. To win	10. Sport was boring
	11. Overemphasis on winning
Sample: 2,000 boys and 1,900 girls, grades 7-12, who identified a "best" school sport. Answers above were among 25 responses rated on a five-point scale.	Sample: 2,700 boys and 3,100 girls who said they had recently stopped playing a school or non-school sport. Answers above were among 30 responses rated on a five-point scale.

Figure 2.1

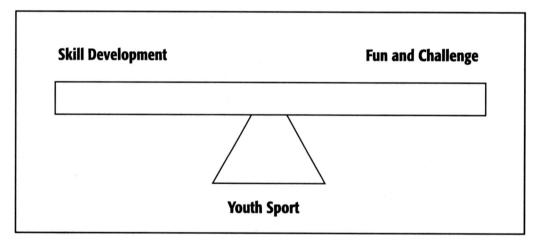

Figure 2.2—Youth Sport Balance

The *Bill of Rights for Young Athletes* was developed by the National Association for Sport and Physical Education's Youth Sports Task Force, which is comprised of medical experts, sports scientists, and national youth sports officials. Youth basketball programs should be designed to ensure that players receive these rights.

Bill of Rights for Young Athletes

- Right to participate in sports.
- Right to participate at a level commensurate with each child's maturity and ability.
- Right to have qualified adult leadership.
- Right to play as a child and not as an adult.
- Right to share in the leadership and decision-making of sport participation.
- Right to participate in a safe and healthy environment.
- Right to proper preparation for participation in sports.
- Right to an equal opportunity to strive for success.
- Right to be treated with dignity.
- Right to have fun in sports.

Therefore, sport educators play the key role in designing youth sport programs that are appropriate for all children. However, parents also need to ensure that programs for their children satisfy these requirements. Specifically, youth basketball programs need to be organized to set and maintain standards that ensure enjoyment and success for all players.

Youth basketball should focus on:

- players—first
- playing—for all (each practice and each game)
- play—that is fun or satisfying

Basketball rules for children and youth need to be modified to:

- enhance the enjoyment of participation
- meet the developmental needs of each participant
- promote effective skill improvement
- prevent the development of poor mechanics in movement (e.g., when the ball is too big or the basket too high)
- improve the chances for individual success in the sport—children seldom continue to play sports in which they perceive themselves as being ineffective
- enhance the possibilities that each participant actively develops an appreciation for the game

This chapter develops recommendations for sport educators to modify the rules of basketball for children and youth. These modifications will allow you to develop appropriate programs centered upon *players, playing,* and *play.* Changes will be discussed in the areas of: participation, skill, safety, playing area, contest length, equipment, matching players and teams, and special participants. We will look at rules modifications for three basic age groups for basketball:

Ages	Grade level
5 – 7	K – 3
8 – 10	4 – 6
11 – 12	7 – 8

Modifications should be considered for individuals on both ends of the developmental spectrum (i.e., early and late maturers). Also, special situations need to be recognized near the upper end of the youth category (ages 12–13/grade 9), where the greatest gender differences occur and where significant growth and development takes place. The most common classifications occur at grades 4–6 and grades 7–8.

Participation

Playing Time

The first recommendation is that players come first, focusing on assurance of playing time for all participants and that play is enjoyable or satisfying. Assurance of playing time can be accomplished by the following rule modifications:

- minimum time per player per contest
- playing time during each period
- equal playing time for all

Exceptions should be developed for illness and injury situations. Coaches should also be urged to comply with the spirit of the rule—give each player a meaningful role and real playing time.

Recommendation #1

Minimum time played per contest sets a baseline percentage to satisfy (e.g., 25% of contest time (six minutes) of a 24-minute game or 33% (about 11 minutes) of a 32-minute game. This suggestion requires coaches to keep track of time played during competition. This technique can be applied to all age levels, and it guarantees that each player will play a significant period of time each game—coaches should allow players a chance to play during each half.

Recommendation #2

Giving each player the chance to play during each period (usually each half) is easier to track, but you must ensure that the player's playing time is more than a token appearance. This consideration can be done by requiring a minimum time (e.g., three minutes per appearance).

Preferred Recommendation

Each player should get a playing time guarantee of at least two minutes during each quarter of play at all levels of competition. No player should play the whole period unless team rosters are small—each player should come out of the game at least two minutes per quarter.

Going Beyond

Some leagues that prefer to focus on *equal development time for each player* could develop a rule that guarantees equal time for all. Dividing the team into two balanced squads and playing them an equal amount of time would usually accomplish equal time for all. This rule is done by splitting half of each period or alternating quarters. Five-on-five leagues would have 10-player teams while three-on-three competition would have six players per squad.

Ages and Heights

Classifications of competition for youth basketball should use the age-related factor as the primary determinant. Exceptions should be made for physical and psychological growth and development extremes in each group. Also, an exception might be made for players with advanced skills and also for taller players in a classification.

Recommendation

Develop competition classifications that are age-related with approved exceptions for extremes in maturation and height. Exceptions would only be approved by the administrator after consultation with the player, parents, and coaches.

Going beyond

A separate classification should be considered for age 13/grade 9 participants when significant maturation differences exist, enough participants are at the upper end of the age 11–12/grade 7–8 classification, or when they might be combined with a 13–14 (freshman/sophomore) grouping.

Skill

To give players the best opportunity to improve their skills and optimize their chance for success, sports administrators must place primary emphasis on *fun* and *fun*damentals. Coaches should be required to develop the fundamental skills of basketball: footwork (stance and steps); ballhandling (dribbling, passing, and catching); shooting; rebounding; and individual defense.

Individual Skills

For ages 5–7, the beginner category, the footwork and defensive rules can be modified to enhance learning and improve chances for individual success.

Recommendation

Ages 5–7 playing rules should be modified to:

- allow an extra step for starting or stopping with the ball (i.e., modify the traveling rule)
- not to allow the ball being held by the ball handler to be touched by the defense—they may steal the ball when it is passed or dribbled, but they may not block shots or touch the ball when the ball handler is holding the ball
- not call for three-second lane, five-second out-of-bounds, or 10-second backcourt violations

Rule Support

Basketball players must gradually learn two rule categories: fouls—illegal contact that puts an opposing player at a disadvantage; and violations—ballhandling and time miscues that give the offensive player an illegal advantage.

Fouls include:

- blocking—illegally impeding the progress of an opposing player while still moving
- charging—running into or pushing a stationary defensive player
- holding—illegal use of the hands/arms to restrict an opponent's movement

- tripping—illegal use of feet/legs when playing defense to hinder an offensive player's motion.

Violations include:

- double dribble—resuming dribbling after having stopped dribbling
- traveling—the ball handler taking more than one step without dribbling
- Five seconds inbounds—failing to pass the ball from out-of-bounds within five seconds from the time the ball is received from the official
- Three seconds in the lane—an offensive player in the free-throw lane of the front court for three or more seconds with the ball
- Ten seconds in the backcourt—the offensive team taking more than 10 seconds to advance the ball to the front court

Recommendation

Ages 8 – 11 playing rules should be modified to:

- allow a liberal interpretation of the traveling rule (allow an extra step)
- not call for three-second lane, five-second out-of-bounds, or 10-second backcourt violations

Going Beyond

Leagues that choose to speed up the development of the critical offensive skills of passing and catching should add a modified dribbling rule—a maximum of three bounces per dribble before passing or shooting. For beginners, the ball is a magnet on offense, and special provisions must be made to encourage passing and catching skills. 'Pass first, dribble last' is a coaching rule that should be emphasized.

Team Skills

All players and teams in youth basketball should learn the basic defensive skills that are essential to all defensive systems. This can only be accomplished by a rule that requires the use of player-to-player defenses and modifying the level of defense to accommodate limitations on ballhandling skills of younger players.

Recommendation — Type of Defense

All age groupings and teams should use only player-to-player defenses through age 12 or 13 (about grade 8). They need to be taught all basic defensive situations: on the ball, off the ball, off to on the ball, on to off the ball, and rebounding. The only exception to this rule that administrators and coaches should consider would be for the fourth quarter of games, where coaches/teams might be allowed other defensive choices (possibly the last two minutes). Remember, the 5–7 age category cannot touch the ball or block shots on the ball handler.

Recommendation — Level of Defense

The first two age groupings should only be allowed to play half-court level defenses. The 11–12 age levels could be allowed to play three-quarter and full-court defensive schemes, but only player-to-player type and during the last period of play.

Rule Support

Age Groupings	Defensive Rule Modification
5–7	• player-to-player defense only
	• defender on the ball—can't touch the ball or block shots
	• start defense at half-court or less
8–10	• player-to-player defense only
	• start defense at half-court or less
11–12	• player-to-player defense primarily
	• start defense at three-quarter or full-court in final period of play.

Going Beyond

Competition leagues in the most mature category (11–12) could allow teams to play other types of defense during the second half of each game. If teams are primarily made up of players well-grounded in player-to-player defensive fundamentals, this playing rule modification could be made to prepare players for other defensive strategies found in secondary school level competition.

Safety

Sport educators should recognize a moral and legal responsibility to provide for the physical and emotional safety for all players. This standard should include:

- creating the safest possible environment for players with a proactive, preventative approach
- having coaches provide both general and specific supervision of players during practices and games
- protecting from legal liability situations by prudent risk management
- providing emergency first aid to players who are injured.

Recommendation

For all divisions, sport educators are responsible for having coaches file a facility and apparel report before each competition.

Rule Support

The facility and apparel inspection report should include:

- basket/backboard/support system
- padding on floor-based support systems
- playing court
- wall padding behind basket
- proper fitting basketball socks and shoes
- strapped eyeglasses and goggles
- no jewelry
- proper fitting uniform

Recommendation

Sport educators of all leagues should develop and implement a risk management program.

Rule Support

The risk management should require all sport educators to have:

- preseason physical exam for all players

- progressive physical conditioning program
- apparel and facilities inspection
- matching of athletes and teams by age-related categories
- warnings of the inherent risks of competition given in writing to each player and their parents
- proper warm-ups and cool-downs
- general and specific supervision: general supervision means that the coach is present at all times at the site of practices and games; specific supervision is needed during active play/practice to closely observe and evaluate player participation
- written records (a paper trail) of season plans, practice plans, and player injuries
- emergency plan for injuries—league rules should require each coach to have CPR/first aid training
- properly plan the activity
- provide proper equipment

Recommendation

Age groups 5–7 and 8–10 should not be allowed to take the defensive charge. Coaches should not teach this contact skill until ages 11–12 and then only in a complete skill progression from falling down backwards to being knocked down by a moving opponent. No contact should be allowed by defenders on an unmolested lay-up by an offensive player.

Recommendation

Unsportsmanlike conduct of any kind should not be tolerated. The byword for youth basketball should be *respect*; build it in each player and earn it from others. Rough play should not be tolerated.

Rule Support

- no defender can intentionally get in the path of an offensive player to take a defensive charge in age groups 5–7 and 8–10
- no defender should be allowed to undercut an offensive player shooting an uncontested lay-up
- the unsportsmanlike play rule should result in an automatic technical foul (two free throws and ball possession) or required removal of the player from the game and coach counseling

Playing Area

The playing court shown in Figure 2.3 of 84 feet by 50 feet (high school) and 94 feet by 50 feet (college) is inappropriate for youth basketball. The length of the court can become a challenge for the youngest age groups (5–7 and 8–10). In this case, consideration should be given to modifying the court area to utilize a smaller playing space. This change can be done two ways: changing to 3-on-3 –half-court basketball competition (more players in the same space); or creating crosscourt game competitions (see Figure 2.3). This plan is possible when side baskets are available. This modification produces two game courts that are 50 feet long by 42 feet (high school) or 47 feet (college) wide.

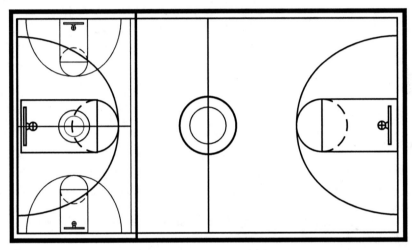

Figure 2.3 – Crosscourt Playing Area

Recommendation

Age 5–7 and 8–10 groups should use 3-on-3–half-court play or compete on crosscourt playing areas. This type of organization is necessary due to the poor dribbling and passing/catching skills at this age level. This size court is more appropriate for the physical stamina of younger players. The standard size full-court tends to fatigue younger players and cause severe degrading of fundamental skills. Skill development can progress best on the "short courts" for younger players.

Contest Length

Youth rules for basketball should modify the playing time for games as well as halftime. Time-outs should be allocated once per quarter to facilitate teaching/learning, with one being cumulative.

Recommendation

See Figure 2.4.

Age	Grade	Game Length	Halftime	Timeouts
5–7	1–3	6-min quarters	10 min	1 min long 1 per period
8–10	4–6	6-min quarters	10 min	1 min long 1 per period
11–12	7–8	8-min quarters	10 min	1 min long 1 per period
13–14	9–10	8-min quarters	10 min	1 min long 1 per period

Figure 2.4 — Age, Grade, Game Length, Halftime, Timeouts

Going Beyond

Before a game, both coaches may agree upon an "added play" period; this could be an extra five-minute period during halftime or a fifth quarter following the regular game.

No shot clock should be used in youth basketball at any age level. In fact, for the ages 5–7 group, you should consider not even using a scoreboard.

A "no contest" rule should be established for lopsided contests. In other words, after a "difference limit" is reached, the score should not be kept at all. You can still keep time in those situations, just not the score.

Rule Support

For increased emphasis on development, a league could add these rule modifications for time:

- an agreed upon "added play" period that is used with squad sizes greater than 10 for a 5-on-5 match-up or six for a 3-on-3 match-up to develop the lesser skilled players
- no shot clock for all age levels
- no time and score kept for age 5–7 age category so the focus is on fun and fundamentals

- a "no contest" rule for lopsided contests (when one team is 25 points ahead) where time is kept but not the score. This recognizes the principle that competition is least valuable when teams are unevenly matched.

Equipment

The equipment for youth basketball includes personal apparel and playing equipment. Personal apparel guidelines include shorts, shirts, socks, and properly fitting shoes. Players should be asked to have appropriate basketball playing shoes and socks that will protect the feet and allow them to safely play the game. They are essential in preventing blisters and foot or ankle injuries, as well as allowing for safe and effective movement. Over one-third of basketball injuries involve the ankle and foot. Sport educators should require coaches to check the fit and proper wear and tear of socks and shoes.

The essential basketball playing equipment includes a basketball and basket (backboard and support system). Modifications of both basketball size and basket height are important to give players a reasonable chance to be effective ball handlers and shooters—the critical offensive skills. A sequential, progressive modification of these rules will also prevent the acquisition of poor passing and shooting mechanics that result from a ball that is too large and a basket that is too high.

Administrators should realize that some resistance to these modifications will be received from parents, coaches, and even some players who want to see play take place using the "big players" equipment.

Recommendation

Youth sport basketball rule modifications for ball size, basket height, free-throw line distance, and court size, are summarized in Figure 2.5.

Grade Level	Age	Ball	Basket Height	F-T Line Distance	Court Size
1–3	5–7	#5	7 feet	9 feet	3-on-3 halfcourt
4–6	8–10	#6 (Women's Ball)	8 feet	9 feet	3-on-3 halfcourt or crosscourt
7–8	11–13, 14	#7 (Regular Ball)	9 feet, 10 feet	12 feet, 15 feet	Full court

Figure 2.5 — Youth Basketball Rule Modifications

Rule Support

It is very important that sport educators modify the rules regarding the most critical playing equipment—ball, basket height, free-throw line distance, and court size. This not only enhances proper skill development progression but also aids the player's perception of success and enjoyment of the sport. Thus, it is imperative that all age groupings modify equipment for the:

- ball—small to large
- basket height—7 to 10 feet
- free-throw line distance—9 to 15 feet
- court size—half-court, crosscourt, full-court.

Note: These rule modifications for basketball equipment are the most challenging to make—especially changing ball size and lowering baskets. However, they are most critical for *all* leagues and for all practices/games.

Matching Children to the Sport

Sport educators have the responsibility to match children to teams that will ensure balance and equal competition. Not only does it make sense to provide balanced competition for developmental purposes, but it is also a legal duty for administrators. Remember, the consequences of unequal competition are significant—the players on superior teams are not challenged and can become bored while the inferior teams may have players who will have difficulty building self-esteem and may be more susceptible to injury under these conditions.

Matching of players and teams begins from the foundation of age grouping. Then adjustments are made according to:

- skill extremes—especially dribbling, shooting, defense, and rebounding
- maturation extremes—physical (especially height) and emotional

Skill evaluations should include the basics: footwork, ballhandling, shooting, rebounding, and individual defense. The focus should be on identifying children with low or high skill levels (the extremes) who can be considered for movement from their age group.

Physical maturation extremes should also be considered. Height extremes would be a primary focal point for age group reclassification. General physical abilities such as speed and muscular development might be examined when looking at exceptional players who need to be moved to another group.

Sport educators should also observe emotional maturation variables to see if players are classified appropriately. Here, you would look for unusual behaviors such as timidness, social misbehavior, lack of aggression, or fear of making mistakes, any of which could indicate low self-confidence on one extreme. Likewise, positive traits in this area might be one reason for a child to play in an older age group.

After the sport educator has matched players on the basis of age-related groupings and then considered possible exceptions, individual decisions for reclassification are made only after consulting with coaches, parents, and the affected player. There is often a strong desire by players to stay with their age-related peer group.

Recommendation

Match players by age-related groupings with exceptions considered on an individual case based on skill (low and high), emotional maturation, or physical maturation.

Recommendation

Match teams by blind draft. In other words, have all coaches and administrators construct teams without regard to coach assignment. After teams are matched in final form, conduct a blind draw to match coaches to teams.

Going Beyond

Leagues that want to go the extra mile to balance competition could conduct a blind draft, and assign coaches on a blind draw. Then, each coach could identify two players for possible reclassification on the basis on skill or maturation. The sport educator would then be the final jury for considering any player reassignment.

A rule could also be adopted that greatly enhances balanced competition. Coaches can be required to teach players to play at least two positions, thereby allowing players to explore different roles and learn different skills and also balance teams.

CHAPTER 3

Planning Practices
for Younger Players

"Failing to plan is planning to fail."

— Author unknown

As previously stated, it is recommended that younger players learn basketball more informally than formally through organized competition. It is felt that learning to love a sport is best done by total involvement—playing and learning to play (self-coaching), organizing competition, and officiating. The more players are empowered to carry out these roles of playing, coaching, and officiating, the more likely their interest in, enjoyment of, and love of basketball will be enhanced.

However, when parents and coaches are involved and team practices are carried out, learning is best done with some planning. As the saying goes, "failing to plan is planning to fail." To carry out the coaching role of improving the athlete-learning rate, coaches should be able to organize and administer practices so they are effective (i.e., they accomplish stated goals) and efficient (i.e., they utilize time well). This means getting something meaningful down in writing for each practice.

To plan effective and efficient practices, coaches need to be able to carry out three steps: one, identify and write practice goals and objectives; two, identify fundamental skills and strategies to be taught and put them in sequential order; and three, develop long range (season and weekly) and short range (daily) plans.

Goals and Objectives

Goals are general statements of what players and teams should accomplish during a season. These goals should be identified in each of the following areas:

- fundamental skills—the essential individual skills needed to play basketball
- strategies—the team tactics regarding the fundamentals used to practice and play
- rules—knowledge of basketball officiating and rule boundaries for playing the game
- physical—conditioning for and training to play basketball
- mental—individual behavior and knowledge to play the game
- ethical—the core values such as respect that can be taught through the game

Specific objectives need to be developed for each goal area. Each coach needs to select the most essential objective areas from each general goal. This depends on the age/grade level of the players being coached. Suggested goals and objective areas are listed as follows:

Fundamental skills (individual)

- footwork—stance, starts, steps, turns, jumps, and stops
- ball handling—ball and body, passing and catching, dribbling
- shooting—lay-up shooting, set/jump shooting, free-throw shooting
- rebounding—offense, defense
- defense—stance, steps, on the ball, off the ball (close to ball—closed stance; far from the ball—open stance, post defense), off ball to on ball closeouts, and on ball to off ball movement (jump toward ball and basket)
- setting and using screens
- moves without the ball (V-cuts, L-cuts, back cuts, flare cuts, and fill cuts)

Strategies (team)

- transition—defense to offense (fast break, against pressing defenses)
- set offenses (against player-to-player, zone, and combination defenses)

- special situations (offense and defense)—free throws, jump balls, out-of-bounds
- set defenses—different levels (full-court, half-court) and types (player-to-player, zone, and combination)
- transition—offense to defense (safety and offensive rebounders)

Rules and officiating

The basic rules that provide the boundaries for playing the game at every age level should be taught to all players:

- the playing court and equipment
- officials
- scoring and timing
- starting and stopping play
- free throws
- violations and penalties
- fouls and penalties

Physical

How players get in shape to play the game and basic training tips:

- conditioning
- training
- injuries—preventing and treating

Mental

The other knowledge that coaches feel players need to learn to play and enjoy basketball. For example, many coaches want players and teams to play hard, play smart (a continual process of learning how to play the game), and play together (developing team chemistry and morale and putting the team first). You could include in this goal area ways to make practices and games fun and enjoyable (i.e., working hard to meet progressively tougher challenges).

Ethical

The core values that coaches may emphasize and hope are developed playing the game. One approach to this critical sport area is the one developed and advocated by the National Association of Intercollegiate Athletics (NAIA) called the "Champions of Character, Champions for Life" program.

This program is grounded in five core values:

- respect—treating yourself and others according to the *highest* standards. Apply the Golden Rule (i.e., do unto others as you would have them do unto you) and the Silver Rule (i.e., do not do unto others what you do not want them to do unto you). Build your self-respect and earn the respect of all others.
- responsibility—being accountable to yourself, your team, and the sport of basketball for your actions. Honor the sport with your best efforts. Be a role model of your best conduct and competence.
- integrity—keeping commitments and conforming reality to our words. Develop an integrated character that goes beyond honesty(i.e., do not lie, cheat, or steal).
- servant leadership—putting the team first while also doing and being your best. Serve others while also becoming the best leader you can be.
- sportsmanship—being good (your character) and doing what is right (your actions) in sports. This means developing fair play and justice in sports.

The mission of this character program is to create an environment where every student-athlete, coach, official, and spectator is committed to the true spirit of competition through respect, integrity, responsibility, servant leadership, and sportsmanship. This is an example of a program that is focused on educational sports (see Figure 3.1).

Figure 3.1 – An Educational Sports Core Values Goal Area

After general goals and specific objectives are developed, coaches can then prioritize them and have a basis for season practice planning. An illustration of this would be:

Goal #1

Basketball players will demonstrate the fundamental skills needed to play effectively in games.

Objective #1

Basketball players will demonstrate all basic footwork needed to play basketball at their age and skill level.

Goal #2

Basketball team players will demonstrate all offensive and defensive strategies needed to play effectively in games.

Objective #2

The basketball team and its players will effectively execute player-to-player defense for practices and games at their age and skill level.

Taking all of the objectives and putting them in order of importance (i.e., what to teach in what order, and what is needed to play the first game) is a challenging phase. The most basic skills such as footwork should be taught first.

You might have a list of objectives, some from each goal area, most of them being in the fundamental skills goal area. You would also consult the age/experience level shown later in this book to determine the developmentally appropriate skills for that level. Then, after determining goals and objectives for the six goal learning areas and putting all objectives from all areas in order, you have your season plan and are ready to plan daily practices.

Planning Daily Practices

The combination of your season plan with an assessment of your players' skill and knowledge level allows you to then decide on the time needed for your objectives in each practice.

Some of the essentials for a practice plan are:

- date and length of practice

- theme of practice—emphasis for the day
- equipment needed
- warm-up section
- practice core (review, teaching and drilling of new skills, competition and conditioning)
- cool-down and coach's assessment.

This can be placed on an 81/2" x 11" form or put on a 3" x 5" card to be carried during practice. A sample practice plan is in shown in Figure 3.2.

PRACTICE PLAN
Thursday, October 20 – 4:00 p.m. – 5:30 p.m.

Theme: Respect and footwork (balance and quickness)

Equipment: six balls, scrimmage vests, whistle

Practice

Time	Area	Drills	Coaching Cues
10 min	Warm-up	Stance, steps, and stretching	All joints bent, stay in stance.
15 min	Fundamentals and fast break	Pairs pass and catch – lay-ups – jump shots – 2-on-1	Pass with a ping, two-hand catch.
15 min	Shooting	Pairs – progression – competition	Follow through one full count.
5 min	Free throws	Groove shot in groups	Same ritual.
15 min	Individual and team defense	– stance and steps – 4-on-4 shell	– ball-u-basket – ball-u-player
10 min	Rebounding	– Offense—pairs – Defense (3-on-3)	Go to a gap, physical contact on D, move with and toward the ball.
15 min	Team O & D	Half-court to full-court controlled scrimmage	Get a good shot each time
5 min	Cool-down	Stretch	Coach's comments and assessment.

Assessment/Comments

_____

_____

Figure 3.2 — Practice plan

CHAPTER 4

Coaching is Teaching

"One of the greatest gifts you can give is your best example."

— Jerry Krause

All coaches need to become better teachers by learning how to develop young people through the sport of basketball. Thus, it is helpful to know and apply such laws of learning as:

• Readiness to learn

Players need to be taught appropriate skills at their maturity level. They need to be open to learning and continual growth. All must guard against the close-minded attitudes commonly seen with higher skill levels and greater experience.

• Demonstration of skills

Skills should be demonstrated by coaches, players, or video. Players should imitate the skill demonstrations, and coaches should correct the imitation. Coach demonstrations should be correct and repeated as necessary with clear and concise accompanying explanations plus critical coaching cues emphasized.

When correcting the imitation, coaches should give more information and less emotion. Correct the behavior/performance and not the person. Focus on skills and other goal areas (respect, attitude, effort, knowledge, rules, etc.) Give specific feedback to build confidence and maximize improvement.

- Execution of skills quickly and correctly many times until they become automatic
- Telling players why they need to learn something

For example, focusing on respect allows all players to have fun and build confidence (the reason for respect).

Communication

All coaches need to be able to communicate well in order to teach players the game of basketball. This includes the guidelines of:

- Earning player respect

Establishing credibility with your players is a product of what you know and what you do. It helps to be positive, knowledgeable about basketball, and consistent.

- Developing all communication skills (reading, writing, speaking, listening, and non-verbal)

Speaking, listening, and the use of non-verbal language are especially important skills in coaching. The least developed areas seem to be listening and non-verbal communication. Listen with respect to players and search for the meaning of what they say. Give full eye contact; become an active listener. As Stephen Covey states, "Seek first to understand before you hope to be understood." Also, become more aware of your non-verbal language (i.e., how you communicate).

- Becoming a good role model

Walk your talk in all areas of your contact with players. Do as you say—your actions on and off the court are important tools for teaching. Actions do speak louder than words. This means that you need to role model all goal areas. It has been said that one of the greatest gifts you can bestow is your best example. This certainly holds true when you apply John Wooden's competition rule to "win with humility and lose with dignity." Remember, your most important role is to develop young people through basketball. You are not just teaching basketball, you are coaching young players to play basketball. Be accountable; prepare and work as hard as you expect your players to work. Be yourself, but be sure it is your best self. Express yourself without the use of profanity—model appropriate communication.

- Insisting on and using direct eye contact when teaching and learning
- Teaching young players—getting to know and understand them

Care about their problems and deal with those problems directly. Make time for your players. Spend time with them before and after practice.

- Teaching in specifics

Players need specific information, which requires critical coaching cues in order to learn better and faster.

- Teaching positively

Tell players what to do rather than what not to do. For example, say, "Start with the lead foot first," rather than "Don't step first with the back foot."

Teaching Tips

Many useful guidelines exist for teaching players to play basketball. Some of these are:

- Practice makes permanent (not perfect).

Thus, it is important to go slow only in the beginning stages of skill learning, and then proceed quickly to focus on doing game moves at game speed.

- You really know skills when you can teach them well.

Involve players in teaching themselves; teach them to take responsibility for their own learning *and* their teammates' learning.

- Develop a proper mentality regarding mistakes.

Mistakes are important for learning as a status and progress report. Allow players to try new things at an uncomfortable pace and make mistakes. Coaches should also take responsibility for their mistakes and be big enough to admit when they are wrong.

- When teaching, use the following three steps:
    → previewing—tell them what you are teaching and why it is important.
    → viewing—teach using coaching cues and the reasons why a skill is important. Focus on only one thing at a time; players learn more by doing than by listening.
    → reviewing—tell them what you taught.
- Focus on fundamentals and fun.

Players (come first), playing (everyone does it), and play (fun or challenging enjoyment).

- Use the following teaching progressions:
    → slow to fast
    → basic to advanced

- → old skills to new skills

- → simple to complex

- → individual to team

- Give feedback to your players.

Feedback includes not only what they need to correct but also, and more importantly, what they are doing correctly. Feedback can improve the rate of learning, but it must be appropriate, specific, and generally information-based (not always emotional). Giving feedback is one of the most important teaching tools; use it in a positive way by focusing on the critical coaching cues. Other feedback guidelines are:

- → Correct the early learning of skills with frequent feedback. Then, gradually reduce the frequency so that players do not rely on the coach.

- → The amount of information that coaches use in their feedback should decrease as the complexity of the skill increases.

- → Feedback about the general direction of a player's errors is more useful than feedback about the magnitude of their errors.

- → Instantaneous feedback can impede learning because it hinders the player's internal feedback processing (i.e., how it felt) and development of error detection capability. Thus, it is often useful to allow time for processing before giving feedback to the athlete.

- → Prescriptive feedback that informs the players about specific changes to make in their movements is more effectual than descriptive feedback that merely notifies players about the mistakes they made. Tell them specifically what corrections to make.

CHAPTER 5

Fundamental Skills

"Leadership is going where nobody else has gone."

— Bob Galvin

In this chapter all fundamental skills are listed and described. Appropriate critical *Coaching Cues* are also listed with each skill area. The following chapters (6-10) then identify the age-appropriate basic skills to develop at each level.

Footwork

All positions for movement and body movements needed to play basketball. Footwork consists of stance, starting, stepping, turning, jumping, and stopping.

Stance

The basic body position needed for a quick movement.

Coaching Cues: Weight is on the whole foot, all joints are bent, and arms are close to the body.

Figure 5.1 – Offensive triple threat   Figure 5.2 – Defensive stance

❏ *Offensive Stance (Triple Threat)*

The player in possession of the ball who hasn't dribbled (live ball). The dominant foot is forward in a toe-to-instep relationship with the non-dominant foot. Feet are shoulder width apart. All joints are bent with the head up and over the base with the back erect. The ball is placed on the dominant side of the body near the armpit.

Coaching Cues: The player should "pit and protect" the ball (pull ball toward armpit) and be ready to pass, shoot, or dribble from this position.

❏ *Defensive Stance*

Similar to the offensive stance but with the feet moving slightly (active feet) and arms bent at the elbows.

Coaching Cues: Active feet and hands.

Starting

Quick movements in any direction with the body and eyes generally facing the action.

❐ *Offensive Starts*

With the ball, the front foot is the first step taken for a quick start.

Coaching Cues: Front foot first.

• Direct drive

A dribbling move, generally toward the basket, by the defender on the dominant side (Figure 5.3 a, b).

Coaching Cues: The player takes a straight line to the basket and brushes shoulders with the defender as he lowers the inside shoulder.

Figure 5.3a – Triple threat start   Figure 5.3b – Direct drive (long first step)

• Crossover drive

A dribble by the defender on the non-dominant side (Figure 5.4 a-c).

Coaching Cues: Circle tight (move the ball from the dominant side to the non-dominant side), step straight toward the basket, lower the shoulder next to the defender with a long first step.

Figure 5.4 – Crossover drive

Figure 5.4a – Triple threat

Figure 5.4b – Circle tight to opposite shoulder

Figure 5.4c – Crossover drive step
(right foot)

- Rocker drive

Short jab-step, triple threat, go to the basket (Figure 5.5 a-c).

Coaching Cues: Quick first step fake, return to triple threat and long drive step.

Figure 5.5 – Rocker drive

Figure 5.5a – Short jab-step

Figure 5.5b – Triple threat

Figure 5.5c – Drive to the basket

- Lift (shot fake) and drive

A ball fake of a shot followed by a dribble drive move (Figure 5.6 a, b).

Coaching Cues: One-inch shot fake (tightening your game), drive against the defender's momentum.

Figure 5.6 – Shot fake and drive

Figure 5.6a – Triple threat start

Figure 5.6b – Short shot fake

Stepping

Moving the body for basketball skills.

❏ *Running*

Movement generally in a forward direction that requires being quick at the right time (i.e., a change of pace—slow to quick).

- Change of pace

Running forward slowly followed by a quick burst of speed.

Coaching Cues: Slow to quick.

- Stutter steps

Slowly moving forward with very short, quick shuffle steps.

Coaching Cues: Short, choppy steps.

- High knees, high heels

Running forward slowly emphasizing either bringing the knees up or the heels to the buttocks.

Coaching Cues: Quick feet.

❏ *V-cutting, offensive zigzag, or a 90-degree change of direction*

A "fake and break" move by an offensive player without the ball. Used to get open, get by an opponent, or to use a screen (Figure 5.7 a, b).

Coaching Cues: A slow to quick move, plant weight on the outside foot, step in a new direction at a right angle.

Figure 5.7 – Offensive zigzag/V-cut move

Figure 5.7a – V-cut set-up (start)

Figure 5.7b – V-cut finish
(step at 90 degrees)

❏ *180-degree Change*

A complete reversal of directions in running (Figure 5.8 a-c).

Coaching Cues: Weight is on the back heel; double pivot and go in the opposite direction.

Figure 5.8 – 180-degree reverse direction move

Figure 5.8a – Running toward baseline

Figure 5.8b – Stride stop to change direction (sit on heel)

Figure 5.8c – Reverse direction 180 degrees

Turning (Head Level)

A legal pivoting movement around one stationary foot (actually the ball of the foot), with or without the ball and on offense or defense.

❏ *Front Turn*

Using the left or right foot as the pivot foot and turning so as to move the front of the body to the front (Figure 5.9 a, b).

Coaching Cues: "Punch" into the turn; take the front of the body to the front.

Figure 5.9 – Turn/pivot

Figure 5.9a – Quick stop/triple threat (start) Figure 5.9b – Front turn – right-hand punch (left pivot foot)

❏ *Rear Turn*

Using the left or right foot as the pivot foot and turning so as to move the rear of the body to the rear—also called a reverse turn (Figure 5.10 a, b).

Coaching Cues: Lead with the elbow; take the rear to the rear.

Figure 5.10 – Turn/pivot

Figure 5.10a – Triple threat facing away from the basket

Figure 5.10b – Rear turn facing the basket (left pivot foot) — lead with left elbow

Jumping

Vertical movements from one or two feet to carry the body upward in rebounding, shooting, catching, and defending.

❐ *One Foot*

Running forward to jump by taking off from one foot and lifting the opposite knee high in a vertical movement.

Coaching Cues: Stamp the take-off foot, high knee of the opposite foot, high jump— not long jump (Figure 5.11 a, b).

❐ *Two feet*

Running forward and landing with a quick (jump) stop to take the body in a vertical direction (Figure 5.12).

Figure 5.11 – One-foot jumps

Figure 5.11a – Plant step (left leg)

Figure 5.11b – Opposite foot/
hand up

Figure 5.12 – Quick stop into a two-foot jump

Coaching Cues: Stamp both feet, swing arms into jump, go up "tall and small" with both hands (Figure 5.13a); come down "big and wide" with both feet—feet wider than shoulder width, (Figure 5.13 b).

Figure 5.13 – Two-hand/two-foot jump

Figure 5.13a – Jump up
"tall and small"

Figure 5.13b – Come down
"big and wide"

Stopping

Bringing the body to a halt with or without the ball and landing on one foot first, both feet at once, or on one foot and then both feet at once.

❏ *Quick (Jump) Stop*

Hop from one foot and land on both feet at once (Figure 5.14 a, b).

Coaching Cues: Hop from one; glide close to the floor into one count landing on both feet (whole foot contact).

Figure 5.14 – Quick stop (one count)

Figure 5.14a – Hop from one foot

Figure 5.14b – Land on both feet at once

❏ *Stride Stop*

Land on one foot first, and then the other in two counts.

Coaching Cues: Two-count stop, weight on back foot (Figure 5.15).

Figure 5.15 – Stride stop

❏ *Triple Stop*

Land on one foot and hop to a quick stop (neither foot may then act as a pivot foot). This unusual, but legal, move is shown in Figure 5.16 a-c.

Coaching Cues: Hop from one (foot touching floor); land on two feet at once (can't pivot).

Figure 5.16 – Triple stop

Figure 5.16a – Catch the ball on one foot

Figure 5.16b – Second foot hop

Figure 5.16c – Quick stop (neither foot pivots)

Ballhandling

When a player has the ball and moves the ball around the body, passes, catches, or dribbles the ball.

Passing (Air and Bounce, Left and Right)

Throwing the ball to another player with one or two hands using a variety of techniques.

Coaching Cues: Pass with a ping (not too soft or too hard), to a target, and with feet on the floor.

❏ *One Hand*

Using a push pass or baseball pass.

Coaching Cues: Hand behind the ball to palm out and down.

• Push/flick air pass

A one-handed pass with that hand behind the ball and moving from passer to catcher in the air (Figure 5.17 a, b).

Figure 5.17 – Push pass

Figure 5.17a – Push pass – triple threat

Figure 5.17b – Push pass – follow-through

- Spin/bounce

A one-handed pass to the floor and then to the catcher.

Coaching Cues: Bounce the ball about two-thirds of the way to the catcher.

- Baseball (dominant hand only)

A long one-handed pass with the body facing at right angles to the direction of the pass (Figure 5.18 a, b).

Coaching Cues: Throw from the ear (like a baseball catcher); step with the opposite foot (to the throwing hand).

Figure 5.18 – One-handed baseball pass

Figure 5.18a – Baseball pass stance (ball by ear)

Figure 5.18b – Baseball pass follow-through

❏ *Two Hands (Air and Bounce)*

From the chest area or from an overhead position.

- Chest (Figure 5.19 a, b)

Coaching Cues: Pass from a thumbs up to a follow-through, thumbs down position.

- Overhead (Figure 5.20 a, b)

Coaching Cues: Thumbs back to thumbs forward on the follow-through.

Figure 5.19 – Two-handed chest pass

Figure 5.19a – Chest pass start

Figure 5.19b – Chest pass follow-through

Figure 5.20 – Two-handed overhead pass

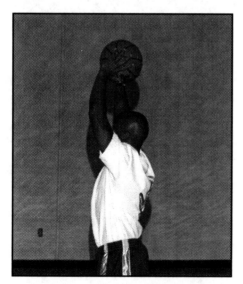

Figure 5.20a – Overhead pass (arms extended-thumbs back)

Figure 5.20b – Overhead pass follow-through (thumbs forward)

Catching

Receiving the ball with the hands.

Coaching Cues: Catch with two hands, with a click, and with hands and eyes.

❏ *Two Hands Directly in the Middle of the Body*

A pass received from in front in the trunk area of the body (Figure 5.21 a, b).

Coaching Cues: Above the waist–thumbs are together; below the waist–thumbs are apart.

Figure 5.21 – Two-handed catching (ball in the middle of the body)

Figure 5.21a – Catching the pass above the waist (thumbs together)

Figure 5.21b – Catching the pass below the waist (thumbs apart)

❏ *One Hand (Block and Tuck) on the Side of the Body*

Catch a pass thrown from the front, but to either side of the body (Figure 5.22 a, b).

Coaching Cues: Block/stop the ball with one hand; tuck to both hands near the chest area.

Figure 5.22 – Two-handed catching (ball to the side of the body)

Figure 5.22a – One-handed block

Figure 5.22b – Two-handed tuck
(under chin)

Ball and Body

Used to assist players in becoming comfortable with the ball, moving the ball in and around the arms, legs, head and trunk (Figure 5.23 a, b).

Coaching Cues: Become one with the ball.

Figure 5.23 – Ball around the body

Figure 5.23a – Around the legs

Figure 5.23b – Around the legs
continued

❐ *Around the Head*

❐ *Around the Trunk*

❐ *Around the Legs*

❐ *Dribble Moves*

Dribbling

Legal bouncing of the ball on the floor with one hand; must be continuous and done without palming the ball (hand on the top or side of the ball).

Coaching Cues: Head and eyes are up (to see the whole floor), finger control, massage the ball.

❐ *Low-power (Figure 5.24 a, b) and Control (Figure 5.25 a, b) (Left and Right, Forward and Back)*

Dribbling near a defender with the body in a basketball stance.

Coaching Cues: Opposite "arm bar" in front of the body for protection of the ball.

Figure 5.24 – Low (power) dribble

Figure 5.24a – Left hand low power dribble

Figure 5.24b – Right hand low power dribble

Figure 5.25 – Low (control) dribble

Figure 5.25a – Left hand low control
dribble

Figure 5.25b – Right hand low control
dribble

❑   *High-speed (Left and Right, Forward) Dribbling*

Used in the open court, legally moving quickly down the court with the ball (Figure 5.26)

Coaching Cues: Push the ball out in front, hand behind or on top of the ball.

Figure 5.26 – High (speed) dribble

❏ *Changes*

The ball is moved on the dribble relative to the body.

• Crossover

From one side of the body to the other (Figure 5.27a).

Coaching Cues: Low and quick movement on the ball change.

Figure 5.27 – Crossover dribble (in front)

Figure 5.27a – Crossover dribble (start)   Figure 5.27b – Finished crossover to left hand

→ Front—a crossover dribble in front of the body and feet (Figure 5.27b).

→ Legs—a crossover dribble between the legs (Figure 5.28 a, b).

Coaching Cues: Best done with near leg (i.e., the leg nearest the ball) forward.

→ Behind—a crossover dribble change from side to side that is done behind the back (Figure 5.29 a, b).

Coaching Cues: Wrap the ball behind the back with hand follow-through that touches the buttocks.

Figure 5.28 – Crossover dribble (between the legs)

Figure 5.28a – Crossover dribble between the legs left to right

Figure 5.28b – Crossover dribble (finish)

Figure 5.29 – Crossover dribble (behind the back)

Figure 5.29a – Crossover dribble behind the back (slap butt)

Figure 5.29b – Finish behind the back dribble to left hand

- Pullback crossover

A low, forward, backward, crossover, and go dribble movement (Figure 5.30 a-d).

Coaching Cues: Move forward in control dribble until stopping when in trouble; back away from the defender, and then go by the defender on the opposite side after a crossover.

Figure 5.30 – Pullback crossover dribble

Figure 5.30a – Low forward dribble – right hand

Figure 5.30b – Low back dribble – right hand

Figure 5.30c – Crossover dribble – to left hand

Figure 5.30d – Explode by the defender

- Head and shoulders regular (left and right)

An "in and out" dribbling move. On the right side, fake left—step left and break right—step right (Figure 5.31 a, b).

Coaching Cues: Use footwork base on a "same side" dribble move after faking a crossover move, a two-step move.

Figure 5.31 – Head and shoulders dribble

Figure 5.31a – Head and shoulders fake – left

Figure 5.31b – Go right

- Head and shoulders crossover (left, right)

Fake the crossover dribble, come back to the ballhandling side, and then use the actual crossover. On the right side—step left/right/left (Figure 5.32 a-c).

Coaching Cues: Three-step move (in-out-crossover).

Figure 5.32 – Head and shoulders crossover dribble

Figure 5.32a – Fake left

Figure 5.32b – Back to right

Figure 5.32c – Crossover to left

- Spin/whirl

A dribbling move combined with a rear turn.

Coaching Cues: Pull ball on the hip; keep the head level.

→ Full—change from one hand to the other in a 90-degree change of direction movement (Figure 5.33 a-c).

Figure 5.33 – Spin/whirl dribble

Figure 5.33a – Right-handed dribble into a quick stop

Figure 5.33b – Rear turn on left foot and change hands

Figure 5.33c – Ball in left hand – explode by the defender

→ Half–fake the spin move halfway and return to the same direction of movement (Figure 5.34 a-c).

Figure 5.34 – Half spin or fake spin dribble

Figure 5.34a – Right-handed dribble

Figure 5.34b – Fake the spin move

Figure 5.34c – Continue right-handed dribble

• Rocker

A hesitation dribble move (Figure 5.35 a-c).

Coaching Cues: A low dribble, with a lifting of the head and hesitation of the ball, then a quick move by the defender.

Figure 5.35 – Rocker/hesitation dribble

Figure 5.35a – Right-handed dribble

Figure 5.35b – Lift head/hesitation

Figure 5.35c – Explode by the defender

Shooting

Tossing or throwing the ball at the basket. The ball must enter the rim from above the basket to be a legal score.

Lay-ups (Left and Right)

Close-in shots to the basket, usually shot off the backboard (bank shots).

Coaching Cues: Two-handed pickup and chin of the ball, high jump to basket, soft touch of ball on backboard.

❑ *One-handed Lay-ups*

Jumping from one foot and shooting with the opposite hand.

• Behind the ball (Figure 5.36 a, b)

Coaching Cues: High and soft on the backboard.

Figure 5.36 – One-handed lay-up (hand behind the ball)

Figure 5.36a – Lay-up hand behind the ball

Figure 5.36b – Finish high off the backboard

- Under the ball (Figure 5.37)

Coaching Cues: Softens shot when moving rapidly.

Figure 5.37 – One-foot lay-up (hand under the ball)

❏ *Two Handed/Power Lay-ups*

Jumping from two feet after a quick stop and shooting the ball (Figure 5.38 a, b).

Figure 5.38 – Power lay-up

Figure 5.38a – Quick stop
(toes to baseline)

Figure 5.38b – Two-foot jump for power
lay-up

❏ *Reverse*

Moving under the basket and shooting a lay-up back and over the head (Figure 5.39).

❏ *Hook*

A lay-up shot off the backboard when moving across the free-throw lane (Figure 5.40).

Figure 5.39 – Reverse lay-up   Figure 5.40 – Running hook lay-up

❏ *Running One-hander*

A lay-up shot over a defender when moving down the free-throw lane and within 6 to 10 feet from the basket (Figure 5.41).

Coaching Cues: Shoot over defender, use near the basket.

Figure 5.41 – Running one-hander

Three-point Shot

A field goal attempt taken from behind the three-point arc.

❏ *Footwork*

• Quick stop

Using a one-count stop in preparation for the shot (Figure 5.42 a, b).

Coaching Cues: One count—a quicker shot that requires more strength.

Figure 5.42 – Three-point shot (quick stop)

Figure 5.42a – Quick stop for a three

Figure 5.42b – Shooting the three

• Plant and pivot

Shot preparation using a two-count move (Figure 5.43 a, b).

Coaching Cues: Two count—more leg power and momentum for longer shots.

Figure 5.43 – Three-point shot (plant and pivot)

Figure 5.43a – Left foot ready to plant

Figure 5.43b – Front turn into triple threat for a trey

❐ *From Pass*

• Fast break

Shooting a three-point shot on the completion of a rush down the court.

• Skip

Shooting the three-point attempt from a side-to-side crosscourt pass.

Coaching Cues: Side-to-side pass over the defense or when the defense doesn't get back quickly.

• Screens

A three-point shot obtained by a teammate blocking the path of a defender.

• Penetrations/drives

A shot attempt obtained when defenders sag or collapse to help on a dribble drive.

❑ *From Dribble (Quick Stop, or Plant and Pivot)*

• Fast break

The dribbler rushes the ball down the court and shoots the "trey."

• Drives

A "trey" taken by the dribble driver.

• Screens

The dribbler shoots a "trey" coming off a teammate's screen.

Set/Jump Shots

Most midrange shots taken with the feet set facing the basket, shooting with one hand. Taken directly from the floor (set shot) or after jumping in the air (jump shot).

❑ *FG Progression*

• Slams

Stopping the ball with both hands to feel the ball hitting the whole shooting hand (Figure 5.44).

Coaching Cues: Ball on whole hand.

Figure 5.44 – Ball slams with both hands

- Form (one hand)

Shooting a "perfect mechanics" shot in the air without a target, balance or guide hand near the ball, but not touching it, and holding the follow-through until the ball hits the floor (Figure 5.45 a-c).

Coaching Cues: Hold the ball in front of the body in whole shooting hand; "lock and load" the ball to shooting pocket (elbow up and in, in front of wrist); exaggerate to full follow-through (make a parachute—firm but relaxed).

Figure 5.45 – Field goal progression

Figure 5.45a – Form shooting – hold the ball in front of the body with the shooting hand

Figure 5.45b – Lock and load ball to shooting pocket

Figure 5.45c – Exaggerate to a full follow-through

→ Without the ball—swing shooting arm or lying on back working on the follow-through (Figure 5.46 a-c).

Figure 5.46 – Form shooting

Figure 5.46a – Swing the shooting arm
– start back

Figure 5.46b – Swing arm forward

Figure 5.46c – Lock and load to
shooting pocket without ball

➜ With the ball—lock and load the ball while lying on back working on the follow-through (Figure 5.47 a, b).

Coaching Cues: For proper follow-through, ball must go at least four to six feet above floor.

Figure 5.47 – Check the follow-through

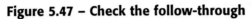

Figure 5.47a – Back on the ground with a ball, lock and load

Figure 5.47b – Exaggerate the follow-through

- Wall or partner shooting

Let the ball hit the floor while holding the follow-through.

- Killer/soft touch shots (five spots)

Close shots taken from six feet, from five different spots: baseline, 45 degrees, front, 45 degrees, baseline.

Coaching Cues: Stay close to the basket.

➜ One hand (Figure 5.48 a-e)

Coaching Cues: Balance or guide hand near the ball, but not touching; try for a "swish" shot.

Figure 5.48 – Killer/soft touch shots (one or two hands)

Figure 5.48a – Baseline right

Figure 5.48b – 45 degrees right
(backboard shot)

Figure 5.48c – Middle of lane

Figure 5.48d – 45 degrees left
(backboard shot)

Figure 5.48e – Baseline left

→ Two hands (Figure 5.49 a-c)

Coaching Cues: Use shooting and guide/balance hand; hold the follow-through one full count.

Figure 5.49 – Circle shots (carry the ball, shoot from five spots)

Figure 5.49a – Carry the ball in shooting pocket

Figure 5.49b – Hop from inside foot

Figure 5.49c – Jump shot

- Circle shots

Shots taken from the five spots while carrying the ball in the shooting pocket and using proper footwork (hop from inside foot and land with a quick stop facing the basket) to shoot a shot moving left (5) and right (5) (Figure 5.50 a-c).

Coaching Cues: Moving clockwise, counterclockwise, hop from basket side foot to take a shot.

Figure 5.50 – Circle shots clockwise

Figure 5.50a – Circle shots going left    Figure 5.50b – Middle shot

Figure 5.50c – Left 45 degrees (off the backboard)

- Shots from pass after pass pickups (footwork with shot fake)

Pass pickups are shown in Figure 5.51 a-c.

Coaching Cues: Pass pickups on a two-handed, underhand pass to self with proper footwork and a shot fake taken as the player moves around the three-point line.

Figure 5.51 – Pass pickups

Figure 5.51a – Two-handed, underhand pass to self

Figure 5.51b – Shot preparation

Figure 5.51c – Pick-up dribble into shot

- Shots from dribble after dribble pickups—proper footwork with shot fake (Figure 5.52 a-c)

Figure 5.52 – Shots from pass

Figure 5.52a – Triple threat fake

Figure 5.52b – Two-handed, underhand pass to self

Figure 5.52c – Quick stop into shot

❐ *Bank/Backboard Shooting*

Coaching Cues: Hit the upper corner of the rectangle when the ball is on the way down; hop from the basket-side foot, one-count follow-through (Figure 5.53 a, b).

Figure 5.53 – Shots from pass

Figure 5.53a – Shot preparation

Figure 5.53b – Finish shot high off the backboard

❐ *Competition Shooting*

After executing shooting skills properly, competition against goals or teammates is introduced.

Coaching Cues: The goal is game shots at game spots at game speed; compete against self or others.

Free-Throw Shot

An unguarded shot attempt taken from the free-throw line (15 feet from the backboard) as a penalty for an opponent's foul.

Coaching Cues: Get on the same spot; perform the same ritual each time; pause at the bottom of the shot; hold the follow-through until the ball touches the net (Figure 5.54 a-d).

Figure 5.54 – Free-throw

Figure 5.54a – Find a spot

Figure 5.54b – Same ritual (deep breath)

Figure 5.54c – Pause at the bottom of the shot

Figure 5.54d – Hold the follow-through

❏ *FT Progression*

One hand soft touch (near the basket), regular routine (halfway distance), and regular FT.

❏ *Grooving the Shot*

Shooting consecutive free throws.

Coaching Cues: Many repetitions are needed to develop muscle memory; shoot without thinking (automatic execution).

❏ *Competition*

Shooting against goals or other players.

Coaching Cues: One shot, 1 and 1 (bonus), two shots, three-shot situations.

Rebounding

Capturing the ball after a missed shot attempt by either team.

Coaching Cues: Assume a miss, two-hands/two-foot technique, both hands up, capture and chin the ball.

Offense

Rebounding when your team shoots the ball (Figure 5.55 a-d).

Coaching Cues: Go to the gap between defenders.

Defense

Rebounding when the opponent's team shoots the ball (Figure 5.56 a-e).

Coaching Cues: Make physical contact after eye contact on opponent; don't watch the ball in flight.

Defending

Preventing the opposing team from scoring by guarding areas of the floor (zone defense) or assigned offensive opponents (player-to-player defense).

Figure 5.55 – Offensive rebound

Figure 5.55a – From the top, swim past the defender (tap left hand)

Figure 5.55b – From the top, get even with the defender by swim with the right hand

Figure 5.55c – From the top, capture rebound

Figure 5.55d – Chin the rebound

Figure 5.56 – Defensive rebound

Figure 5.56a – Pistol stance

Figure 5.56b – See the offensive player (visual until physical contact)

Figure 5.56c – Physical contact (arm bar)

Figure 5.56d – Butt block out

Figure 5.56e – Pursue, capture, and chin the rebound

Stance

Basic ball-you-basket position taken when opponent has the ball.

Coaching Cues: Keep feet active.

❏ *On the Ball*

Ball-you-basket position.

•   Live ball

Dribble not used yet by ball handler (Figure 5.57).

Coaching Cues: Hand near the ball.

Figure 5.57 – Live ball defensive stance

•   Dribbling

Legal movement with the ball.

Coaching Cues: Back hand (thumb in ear); front hand (near ball)—prefer palm up or to inside (Figure 5.58 a-c).

Figure 5.58 – Defend the dribbler

Figure 5.58a – Push step, beginning the defensive step slide

Figure 5.58b – Step with the left foot

Figure 5.58c – Slide the right foot

- Dead ball

After a dribble is discontinued (Figure 5.59).

Coaching Cues: Trace ball—both hands on the ball (stay in stance).

Figure 5.59 – Dead ball defensive stance

❒ *Off the Ball (Closed, Open, Post)*

Ball-you-player guarded position.

Coaching Cues: Body between the ball handler and the player being guarded.

Defensive Steps

Position and movements used in player-to-player defense.

❒ *On the Ball*

A step and slide, or running (when necessary), movement to maintain the ball-you-basket position when the opponent is dribbling.

• Live ball

See previous description at Figure 5.57.

Coaching Cues: Active feet, front hand around the ball.

- Dribbling

See previous description at Figure 5.58 a-c.

Coaching Cues: Step and slide low and wide, run when necessary, defend with feet, body, and hands.

- Dead ball

See previous description at Figure 5.59.

Coaching Cues: Trace the ball with both hands while staying in a good defensive stance.

❐ *Off the Ball*

When guarding an opponent away from the ball.

- Closed/denial stance close to the ball (one pass away)

Near hand is in the passing lane (Figure 5.60).

Coaching Cues: Near hand thumb down, palm facing the ball.

Figure 5.60 – Closed /denial stance (one pass away)

- Open/pistols stance

Used far from the ball—two passes away (Figure 5.61).

Coaching Cues: One arm toward the ball and one arm toward the player guarded (point pistols).

Figure 5.61 – Help side/open stance (two passes away)

- Post stance or defense

Used when guarding an opponent near the free-throw lane; can use a closed stance on the side as shown in Figure 5.62; front as shown in Figure 5.63 (directly between the ball and the opponent); or behind as shown in Figure 5.64 (ball-opponent-you).

Coaching Cues: Generally avoid contact when defending a post; use contact only when in an advantage position (where the offensive post player can't receive the ball readily).

Figure 5.62 – Guarding the post
(closed stance)

Figure 5.63 – Defending the post (fronting)

Figure 5.64 – Defend the post (behind)

❏ *Off the Ball to On the Ball Defense*

When guarding away from the ball and the ball is quickly passed to the assigned opponent (Figure 5.65 a-c).

Coaching Cues: Sprint halfway; get into stance (ball-you-basket position), hands up.

Figure 5.65 – Closeout (off the ball to on the ball)

Figure 5.65a – Help-side pistols stance

Figure 5.65b – Sprint steps to the person you are guarding

Figure 5.65c – Closeout and guard the ball

Defending Screens

When an opponent uses his body to be in the path of the defender and create an open shot. The defender has several choices: go over the screen, go under or behind the screen, get help from a teammate (called hedging), switch assignments with a teammate, or trap the ball handler (two defenders on the ball).

Setting and Using Screens

An offensive team play between two players with or without the ball. One player gets in the path of the defender (screener) and the other player cuts around the screen to get open (cutter using the screen).

On the Ball (Screen For the Ball Handler)

❏ *Defense Not Switch—Ball Handler Shot*

Coaching Cues: Be ready to shoot coming off the screen.

• Lay-up

The ball handler goes all the way to the basket (Figure 5.66 a-b).

Figure 5.66 – Setting and using screens

Figure 5.66a – Screen for the ball handler

Figure 5.66b – Dribble hard off the screen ready to shoot

- Outside shot

Ball handler pulls up for an outside shot off the dribbler.

☐ *Defense Switch*

Screener gets the shot.

- Roll to the basket

Screener goes to the basket with "defender on back" when defensive switch occurs (Figure 5.67 a-c).

Coaching Cues: Half rear turn and shuffle slide to basket when defenders switch.

Figure 5.67 – Set and use screens (defense switch – roll)

Figure 5.67a – Screen set for the ball handler

Figure 5.67b – Defense switches the screen

Figure 5.67c – Screener rolls to the basket

- Step back outside

Screener steps back for an outside shot when opponents switch and collapse on the ball handler (Figure 5.68).

Coaching Cues: Pop outside ready to shoot when defenders switch assignments.

Figure 5.68 – Set and use screens (step back for the shot)

Off the Ball (Screener, Cutter)

❏ *Cuts*

- Pop/fill

Defender attempts to fight over screen and can't get through (Figure 5.69 a-c).

Coaching Cues: Defender caught on screen—the cutter gets outside shot, the screener moves inside near basket.

- Curl

A circle motion around the screen and to the basket (Figure 5.70 a, b).

Coaching Cues: The defender trails the cutter moving around the screen; the cutter goes to the basket; the screener pops to the ball for an outside shot.

Figure 5.69 – Off the ball screen (pop cut)

Figure 5.69a – Swing basketball with proper spacing

Figure 5.69b – Set a down screen

Figure 5.69c – Pop cut – defender fights and can't get through the screen

Figure 5.70 – Off the ball cut (curl cut)

Figure 5.70a – Defender trails the cutter moving around the screen

Figure 5.70b – Cutter curls to the basket and the screener pops out for a shot

• Flare

The defender anticipates and goes to "pop cut" location so the cutter "flares" outside for a shot (Figure 5.71 a-c).

Coaching Cues: The defender goes to "pop" spot so cutter gets outside "flare" shot while the screener cuts inside to the basket.

Figure 5.71 – Off the ball screen (flare cut)

Figure 5.71a - Set down screen

Figure 5.71b – Defense anticipates and jumps to ballside of the screen

Figure 5.71c – Cutter flares outside for a shot

- Back

On overplay of defender, cutter goes to the basket for a lay-up or inside shot (Figure 5.72 a, b).

Coaching Cues: The defender fights through the screen and denies/overplays the pass, so the cutter backcuts to the basket for a shot as the screener pops outside for a shot.

Figure 5.72 – Off the ball screen (back cut)

Figure 5.72a – Set down screen and defense overplays

Figure 5.72b – Cutter backcuts to the basket and the screener pops to the ball

❒ *Screener Reacts Opposite Cutter Moves (Figure 5.73)*

Coaching Cues: Two scoring options on every screen.

Figure 5.73 – Two scoring options

Post Moves

Inside offensive play with back to the basket. Usually taken around the free-throw lane and commonly near the second free-throw lane space.

Getting Open/Positioning

"Posting up" or getting open to catch a pass from the outside feeder (Figure 5.74 a-c).

Coaching Cues: V-cut or spin move (Figure 5.75a-c) to get open or "post up."

Receiving the Ball

Basketball stance lower and wider; create contact on the defender with lower body, both hands up as targets, upper arms horizontal at shoulder level (Figure 5.76 a, b).

Coaching Cues: Two-hand targets capture and chin to power position (ball near chest and under chin).

Figure 5.74 – Post getting open (V-cut)

Figure 5.74a – Running across lane

Figure 5.74b – V-cut move

Figure 5.74c – Post getting contact and position

Figure 5.75 – Post getting open (spin move)

Figure 5.75a – Cutting across lane

Figure 5.75b – Spin in front of defense

Figure 5.75c – Post in front of defense

Figure 5.76 – Post stance

Figure 5.76a – Low/wide basketball stance

Figure 5.76b – Chin ball near chest and under chin

Scoring Moves

❒ *Face/Jump Shot Move*

Turn and face the basket for "live ball" moves (shot or drive) (Figure 5.77 a-c).

Coaching Cues: Use when defender plays behind.

Figure 5.77 – Post move (catch and face)

Figure 5.77a – Catch ball and chin it

Figure 5.77b – Turn and face the basket

Figure 5.77c – Going into jump shot

❐ *Power Move*

Used when a defender plays on the side and contact is created (Figure 5.78 a-c).

Coaching Cues: Half rear turn seal of the defender (defender on hip), two-handed dribble bounce and two-foot hop, power or jump hook shot to score.

Figure 5.78 – Post move (power)

Figure 5.78a – Catch and chin the ball

Figure 5.78b – Step and dribble/hop

Figure 5.78c – Toes to baseline and
power shot

❐ *Jump Hook*

One of the primary scoring moves for an inside player, a shot taken with side facing the basket and the ball on the outside shoulder as the player jumps from two feet and shoots the ball directly overhead (Figure 5.79 a-c and Figure 5.80 a-c).

Coaching Cues: Chin ball on outside shoulder; point inside shoulder at basket, shoot the ball overhead, one-count follow-through.

Figure 5.79 – Jump hook

Figure 5.79a – Catch and chin (right hand)

Figure 5.79b – Begin left shoulder pointing at basket

Figure 5.79c – Right hand hook shot overhead

Team Strategies

Offensive and defensive group tactics used in special situations such as fast-break and zone offense.

Fast Break (Offense/Defense)

❏ *2-on-1*

Two offensive players outnumber one defensive player near the basket (Figure 5.81).

Coaching Cues: Split the floor and stay 15 to 18 feet apart; goal is to score a lay-up.

Figure 5.80 – Post move (power to jump hook)

Figure 5.80a – Power move to the middle

Figure 5.80b – Inside right shoulder points at the basket

Figure 5.80c – Left hand jump hook shot overhead

Figure 5.81 – 2-on-1 fast break

❐ *3-on-2*

Three offensive players and defenders in tandem position (Figure 5.82).

Coaching Cues: The middle offensive player with the ball reads the move of the defender closest to the basket and passes opposite.

Figure 5.82 – 3-on-2 fast break

Zone Defense

Defenders guard floor areas and players in those areas.

❐ *Perimeter*

Outside positions.

•   Reversals/second side

Moving the ball to one side of the floor and quickly reversing the ball to a second side.

Coaching Cues: Attack the second side of zone defenses; move the ball quickly, and then attack after a ball reversal.

•   Turn backs

Fake to one side and pass in the opposite direction.

Coaching Cues: Use turnbacks against zones, as the defenders are ball oriented.

- Dribble down

Dribble usually at a teammate on one side of the floor.

- Push

A move when an offensive player moves into another offensive player's area.

- Loop

On a push, the player clears the area and loops inside to the original position of the dribbler.

❏ *Post*

- Partner post moves

Two inside players work together, e.g., one low post with the ball, partner moves high.

- Drive reaction moves

Players without the ball reacting to get open on a teammate's dribble drive move.

- Step outs

Short moves outside the lane by inside post players; can be to "short corner" or drive reaction moves.

- Slips

When an inside player screens and then makes a quick cut to the basket for a scoring pass.

CHAPTER 6

Lower Elementary Fundamental Skills (Grades K-3)

"It is important that we find something worthwhile to enjoy."

— Jerry Krause

At the lower elementary level, basketball programs should be designed to whet the appetite and develop a love of the game for the younger player. This view means providing an informal, less organized type of play that is fun and very encouraging. Instruction is centered on lead-up games and activities that form the basis for more organized competition in the upper elementary grade level.

Changing the game for grades K – 3 should include:

* Playing time for every player each period
* Skill
    → individual—allow an extra step for starting and stopping with the ball; defense can't touch the ball when held by the ball handler; no three-second lane, five-second out-of-bounds, or 10-second backcourt time counts
    → team—half-court player-to-player defense used

- Safety
  - → daily facility and apparel check
  - → risk management program
  - → no defensive charges allowed
  - → no contact by defenders on an unmolested lay-up
  - → no unsportsmanlike conduct
- Playing area—3-on-3 half-court only
- Contest length—Six-minute quarters; 10-minute halftimes and one-minute timeouts/period; added play period (fifth quarter); no scoreboard and no contest rule
- Equipment changes—#5 small ball; seven-foot basket height; nine-foot free-throw line distance

Footwork

Stance, Starts, and Stops	Grade Level
Get in an offensive triple threat (TT) stance and start with front foot first	3
Use footwork for direct drive and crossover drive	3
Run a set distance and stop	K
Run and stop on signal	K
Follow the leader	K
Run in a circle and stop on command	K
Run relays with command starts and stops	K

Steps (Dodging and Faking)	Grade Level
Run a set distance and change directions	K
Run around obstacles	1
Run to partner, fake and break, run around them	1
Run to partner, dodge to avoid being tagged	1
Run and dodge a thrown ball	2
Run around and avoid being tagged by dodging and faking	2
Run forward and backward	3
Skip (one foot jump preparation)	3

Turns

	Grade Level
• From a given position, use front and rear turns on command	3
• Pivot away from partner	3
• Run, stop, and pivot away from partner	3

Ballhandling

Passing and Catching

	Grade Level
• Throw a beanbag to self	K
• Throw a large ball to self	K
• Catch a beanbag thrown by partner	K
• Baseball pass with a fleece ball against a wall	K
• Pass and catch a large ball with partner	1
• Pass/catch ball (air bounce) off a wall	1
• Pass/catch ball as it bounces from floor	1
• Bounce a ball to self	1
• Pass to a target (two hand chest)	2
• Pass and catch with partner (vary speeds, targets)	2
• Two-handed bounce pass off floor to wall	2
• Pass/catch ball with partner (air/bounce, one hand and two hands)	2
• Catch ball on the run	3
• One-handed bounce pass off floor to wall	3
• Pass/catch ball with moving partner (air/bounce, one hand)	3
• Baseball pass to wall target with a large ball	3
• Baseball pass/catch with partner using a large ball	3
• Begin to learn 12- to 15-foot spacing when passing and catching	3
• Two-handed chest pass to a moving partner	4
• Two-handed overhead pass/catch against wall	4
• Two-handed overhead pass/catch with a moving partner	5

Ball and Body Moves	**Grade Level**
• Circle head, trunk, leg	3
• Figure eight between legs	3

Dribbling	**Grade Level**
• Two hands–bounce ball to self	K
• One hand–bounce ball to self	K
• Bounce ball on the move	1
• Low control/power dribble to self (forward and back, change hands)	2
• Dribble the ball around obstacles	2
• Dribble the ball around obstacles and change hands	3

Shooting

Lay-ups–Right Hand	**Grade Level**
• One-step lay-up to the basket	3
• Dribble lay-up to basket	3
• Step and one-foot jump without the ball	3
• Step and one-foot jump with the ball	3
• One-step lay-up to wall (push pass)	3

Set Shots	**Grade Level**
• One hand overhead push pass at target on wall	3
• Close in set shot at lower basket with small ball	3

Rebounding

• Capture and chin a ball tossed overhead	3
• Capture and chin a tossed ball near an opponent and turn away using a rear turn	3

Defending

On the Ball | Grade Level

• Get into a defensive stance	2-3
• Get into and maintain a ball-you-basket relationship	2-3
• Defensive zigzag step and slide	2-3
• In pairs, use 1-on-1 offensive and defensive zigzag movement without and with the ball	3

Off the Ball | Grade Level

• Learn the ball-you-player guarding position	2-3
• One pass away from the ball, use a closed/denial stance (including post defense)	2-3
• Two passes away from the ball, use an open/pistols stance	2-3

Summary

Remember, at the K–3 grade level, focus on fun and lead-up activities for later fundamentals. Change the game to ensure many successes for young players. Young players need to become familiar with the game, the ball and ballhandling, and moving/controlling their bodies. Shooting practice is to be done with a #5 small ball at a seven-foot basket and nine-foot free-throw line.

Rebounding is confined to teaching players to capture and chin the ball for protection. Remember that no defender can touch the ball after it is rebounded. Also, no touching of the ball is allowed when it is held or shot by the offensive player (i.e., no blocked shots). Defense is restricted to player-to-player techniques: on the ball (live or dribble) and off the ball.

CHAPTER 7

Upper Elementary Fundamental Skills (Grades 4-6)

"It is a sacred trust: helping to mold character, instill productive principles and values, and provide a positive example to those under my supervision."

— John Wooden, Naismith Basketball Hall of Fame coach

The first real exposure to organized competition is recommended at the 4–6 upper elementary grade level. Physical and emotional maturation has generally taken place sufficiently for basketball to be a developmentally appropriate sport activity.

The basic skills discussed in Chapter 6 for grade levels K–3 should be prerequisites and review skills for the 4–6 age category skills identified in this chapter.

Changing the game for grades 4–6 should include:

- Playing time—for every player each period
- Skill
  - → individual—liberalize the traveling rule, no three-second lane, five-second out-of-bounds, or 10-second backcourt violation
  - → team—primarily player-to-player defense at half-court level

- Safety
  - → daily facility and apparel inspection
  - → risk management program
  - → no defensive charges allowed
  - → no contact by defenders on unmolested lay-ups
  - → no unsportsmanlike conduct
- Playing area—3-on-3 —half-court or short full-court
- Contest length—Six-minute quarters; 10-minute halftime; one-minute timeouts/period; added play period (fifth quarter); no contest rule.
- Equipment changes—#6 women's regulation ball; eight-foot basket height; and nine-foot free-throw line distance.

Footwork

Stance, Starts, Steps, and Stops	Grade Level
• Offensive TT stance – review	4–6
→ direct drive	4–6
→ crossover drive	4–6
• Defensive stance and steps	
→ on the ball (live ball, dead ball)	4
→ off the ball (closed, open)	4–6
→ post defense (side front/closed stance)	4–6
• V-cut/offensive zigzag	4–6
• 180-degree change of direction	4–6
• Quick stop	4–6
• Stride stop	4–6

Turning	
• Rear turn (permanent pivot foot)	4
• Front turn (permanent pivot foot)	5
• Front and rear turns (either pivot foot)	6

Jumping	Grade Level
• One foot, without the ball	4
• Two feet, two hands, without the ball	4

Ballhandling

Passing and Catching	Grade Level
• One-handed push flick pass	5–6
• Two-handed chest pass	4–6
• Two-handed overhead pass	4–6
• One-handed baseball pass	6
• Two-handed catching (middle, side)	4–6
• Ball and body drills (add dribbling around legs)	4–6

Dribbling	Grade Level
• Low power dribble (forward, backward, side change)	4–6
• High/speed dribble (left, right)	4–6
• Changes	
→ crossover (front, legs, behind back)	4–6
→ dribble around obstacles	4–6
→ pullback crossover	6

Shooting
(At Eight-Foot Basket Height)

Lay-ups	Grade Level
• One hand (left, right) from direct dribble drive and crossover dribble drive and from the pass	4–6
• Progression (without the ball; with the ball to wall; one step to basket; dribble/pass to basket)	4–6
• Power lay-ups from dribble	5–6

Set/Jump Shots

	Grade Level
• FG progression (slams, form shots, killer/soft touch shots-from five spots, circle shots, shots from pass/dribble)	4–6
• Set shots from a spot	4
• Set shots from pass/dribble	5–6
• Close-in jump shots from a dribble	6
• Close-in jump shots from a pass	6

Free-Throw Shots

	Grade Level
• FT progression—three feet (one hand); six feet (regular), nine feet (regular)	4–6

Rebounding

Two Hands, Two Feet Capture and Chin Ball

	Grade Level
• Stationary without the ball	4
• Stationary with the ball	4
• Moving with the ball	5–6
• Partner competition with the ball	5–6
• Competition with the ball and turns away from other players	5–6

Defensive Rebounding

	Grade Level
• Eye contact until physical contact	4–6
• Blockout; go to and capture/chin the ball	5–6
• Rebound; turn and face up the floor to pass or dribble	6

Defending

On the Ball	Grade Level
• 1-on-1 pairs offensive and defensive zigzag without ball	4
• 1-on-1 offensive zigzag with ball	4–6
→ start live ball	6
→ defend dribbler	6
→ defend dead ball	6

Off the Ball	Grade Level
• Closed stance (one pass away)	4–6
• Open stance (two passes away)	4–6
• Low post defense—closed stance/side front	4–6
• Post defense—from behind	6

Off the Ball to On the Ball	Grade Level
• 1-on-1 closeouts	5–6

On the Ball to Off the Ball	Grade Level
• Jump to the ball and basket	6

Team Strategies

Pass and Cut, Give and Go	Grade Level
• 2-on-0 with no scoring pass	4–6
• 2-on-0 with scoring pass for lay-up	4–6
• 2-on-2 looking for scoring pass when open	4–6

Catch, Face Basket, and Dribble Drive for Lay-up/Set Shot	Grade Level
• 2-on-0 no score	4–6
• 2-on-0 with score	4–6
• 2-on-2 with dribble drive	4–6

Summary

The 4–6 grade level is the primary initial learning stage for the "fun and fundamentals" approach to learning how to play basketball. The "sacred trust" John Wooden speaks of fosters a valuable beginning experience for younger players.

The game must still be adapted for grades 4–6 to include: playing time for each player during each period and a liberalized traveling rule with no time count violations on restricted team defenses. Safety guidelines are ever present; the playing area is still restricted; and contest length is six minutes, with the possibility of a fifth quarter. The equipment used is a #6 regulation women's ball, and eight-foot basket, and a nine-foot free-throw line.

The basic skills and lead-up activities from K–3 should be incorporated when possible. All skill areas are begun and progressively taught at this grade level—moving from simple to complex, from without the ball to with the ball, and from correct performance to quicker movements close to competition speed. There are still restricted approaches to certain areas:

• Rebounding

Still focused on two hands/two feet technique and capture/chin the ball. Defensive rebounding on the ball is taught and developed.

• Team strategies

Defense is still restricted to half-court player-to-player team defense while offense is centered upon the skill of 1-on-1 moves and 2-on-2 pass and cut or give and go basketball.

CHAPTER 8

Middle/Junior High School Fundamental Skills (Grades 7-8)

"Fundamentals are revealed in competition."

— Curtis Janz

At the middle and junior high level, most schools start to have organized basketball teams and programs. For many young players this may be their first experience with the game of basketball. Others have been exposed to several years of fun and skill development.

Emphasis for coaches:

• All players should be taught and encouraged.

Playing time will not be the same for all; as the better players start to play more, however, no one should be cut. At this young age, it is very difficult for anyone to tell what the maturation level or potential will be for any player.

• Practice time should be used to help develop the individual fundamentals more than team concepts.

Chapter 3 gives an excellent look at practice planning. All players should be taught all fundamentals. It is too early for players to specialize in being a post player or a point guard, even though they may play that position in games.

- Some of the skills listed at this level are repetitious of the previous levels.

It is important that coaches review all the basic skills and build a strong fundamental base. In other words, you should assume they are all beginning players. Work individually before or after practice to spend extra time as needed.

Footwork – Review

Stance, Starts, Steps, and Stops   Grade Level

- Offensive TT stance   7–8
- Defensive stance and steps   7–8

Starting   Grade Level

- Direct drive   7–8
- Crossover   7–8
- Rocker drive   8
- Lift and drive   8

Stepping   Grade Level

- Running
  - → change of pace   7–8
  - → stutter steps   8
- V-cutting – review   7–8
- 180-degree change – review   7–8

Turning – Review   7–8

Stopping   Grade Level

- Quick stop – review   7–8
- Stride stop   7–8
- Triple stop   8

Ballhandling

Passing	Grade Level
• One-handed push/flick air pass – review	7–8
• One-handed push/flick bounce pass	7–8
• Two-handed chest air pass – review	7–8
• Two-handed chest bounce pass	7–8

Catching	
• One hand on the side of the body (block and tuck)	7

Dribbling	Grade Level
• Low power dribble – review	7–8
• High speed dribble	7–8
• Changes	7–8
→ crossover – review	7–8
→ pullback crossover – review	7–8
→ head-and-shoulders/in-and-out	8

Shooting

Lay-ups	Grade Level
• One-handed lay-ups (right and left hand) – review	7
• Two-handed/power lay-ups – review	7–8

Three-point Shot	Grade Level
• Footwork	8

Set/Jump Shots   **Grade Level**

- FG progression (slams, form shots, killer/soft touch shots,
  circle shots, and shots from pass and dribble) – review   7–8

Set/Jump Shots (cont.)   **Grade Level**

- add to FG progression wall or partner shooting   7–8
- Bank shooting   8
- Competition shooting   8

Free-Throw Shot   **Grade Level**

- Grooving the shot   7–8
- Competition   8

Rebounding

                                                                            Grade Level

- Offensive   8
- Defensive   8

Defending

Stance – Review   **Grade Level**

- On the ball   7–8
  → live ball   7–8
  → dribbling   7–8
  → dead ball   7–8
- Off the ball – review
  → closed/denial stance   7–8
  → open/pistols stance   7–8

- → post stance — 7–8
- → off the ball to on the ball – review
- → close-outs — 7–8
- On the ball to off the ball – review
  - → jump to the ball and basket — 7–8

Defending Screens

- Over — 8
- Under — 8
- Hedge and help — 8

Setting and Using Screens

Off the Ball	Grade Level
• Screener	7–8
• Cuts	
→ pop/fill	7–8
→ curl	8
• Screener reacts opposite	
→ pop/fill – flare	7–8
→ curl – fill	8

Post Moves

	Grade Level
• Getting open/positioning	7–8
• Receiving	7–8
• Scoring moves	
→ Face/jump shot move	7–8
→ Power move	7–8

Team Strategies

Fast Break	Grade Level
• 2-on-1	7–8
• 3-on-2	8

Zone Offense	Grade Level
• Perimeter	
→ reversals/second side	7–8
→ turn backs	7–8
→ dribble down	8
• Post	
→ partner post moves	7–8

Summary

Review of all fundamental skills and basic teaching are the most important things at this grade level. These are the key years that prepare young players for success later in their careers. Coaches at this level should not be judged on wins and losses, but on the ability of their players to show competency in the basic fundamentals shown in this chapter. Many players are competing on organized levels for the first time and should be exposed to *fun* and *fundamentals*.

CHAPTER 9

Lower Secondary School Fundamental Skills (Grades 9-10)

"It is not important how much you know.
What is important is what your team knows."

— Lee Reimer, Head coach Purcell High School, Purcell, OK

Basketball becomes more serious at the lower secondary school level. Time dedicated to team building increases; however, the time spent on fundamentals is still very important. The coaches at this level must be dedicated to teaching the fundamentals and should set aside time to work on them each day. As with each level, review of the prior skills is important. This foundation represents the cornerstone of a player's success now and in the future.

Emphasis for coaches:

• Attention, concentration, and intensity

These aspects need to be the same for fundamental drills as they are for team drills and scrimmage time. Fundamental time is not the time for coaches to meet and talk. It should be a time to observe performance and provide feedback the whole practice.

• Review

Take the time to review all fundamentals no matter how basic. Minutes spent early in practice will save you hours later if you build and reinforce that fundamental foundation.

Footwork

Review skills already learned.

Ballhandling

Passing	Grade Level
• Spin/bounce pass	9–10

Dribbling	Grade Level
• Head and shoulders crossover	9–10
• Spin/whirl	9–10
• Rocker	10

Shooting

Lay-ups	Grade Level
• Reverse	9
• Hook	10

Three-point Shot	Grade Level
• Footwork – review	9
• From pass	
→ skip	9–10
→ penetrations/drives	9–10
• From dribble	
→ drives	9–10

Set/Jump Shots	
• Competition shooting	9–10

Defending

Defending Screens	Grade Level
• switch	9–10
• trap	9–10

Setting and Using Screens

On the Ball	Grade Level
• Defense not switch	9–10
• Defense switch	9–10

Off the Ball	Grade Level
• Flare	9–10
• Back	10
• Screener	
→ flare-fill	9–10
→ back-fill	10

Post Moves

Scoring Moves	Grade Level
• Power move	9–10
• Jump hook	9–10
• Facing and jump shot	9–10

Team Strategies

Zone Offense	Grade Level
• Perimeter	
→ push	9–10
→ loop	10
• Post	
→ drive reaction moves	9–10

Summary

Coaches need to be reminded that their job can be made much easier if players have good skills, as they can play through many situations by being fundamentally sound. Hopefully, players come to this grade level with a foundation and coaches can build the next level of the pyramid. However, coaches have the responsibility to expose each and every player to all of the fundamentals up to this point no matter what level. As the grade level increases, the number of fundamentals decreases, but the players' mastery of these fundamentals should increase. Thus, players progress more and more toward game moves at game speed.

CHAPTER 10

High School Fundamental Skills (Grades 11-12)

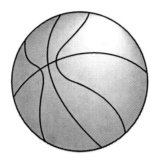

"A team that concentrates on the little things gets better little by little."

— Dan Hays, Head coach, Oklahoma Christian University

Few new skills are introduced at the high school level. However, the success of a high school team may be determined by the players' ability to perform the *complete* list of fundamentals.

Emphasis for coaches:

• Concentration on the little things

Concentrate on quick stops when players catch the ball or good closeouts on defense. The players and teams that concentrate on perfecting the fundamentals continue to improve. You may have to spend time on the most basic triple threat position to be sure they can perform all the other tasks.

• Carryover from drill to drill

If the team is doing a defensive drill, be certain the offensive players are fundamentally sound. For example, they make good chest or flick passes, they catch the ball with a quick stop in triple threat, etc. Make every defensive drill an offensive drill and every offensive drill a defensive drill. Players must transfer fundamentals to games and competition.

Shooting

Lay-ups	**Grade Level**
• Hook	11–12
• Running one hander	11–12

Three-point Shot	**Grade Level**
• From pass	
➔ fast break	11–12
➔ screens	11–12
• From dribble	
➔ fast break	11–12
➔ screens	11–12

Setting and Using Screens

On the Ball	**Grade Level**
• Step back outside	11–12

Team Strategies

Zone Offense	**Grade Level**
• Post	
➔ step outs	11–12
➔ slips	11–12

Summary

This chapter completes a twelve-year building process of fundamental skills. All players like to see themselves improve. Coaches must guide players into seeing the importance of improving fundamentally. In other words, they must teach well and motivate. Along the way players will learn to love the game, have fun, and be competitive. Fun and fundamentals should always be kept in the forefront of a player's quest for excellence.

Fundamental Skills Tables

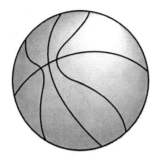

Fundamentals Table (Grades K-3)

Footwork

Stance, starts, and stops
- Start, run, and stops   K
- Triple threat   3
- Direct Drive   3
- Crossover   3

Steps
- Changing directions   K
- Run and dodge   1-2
- Forward-backward   3
- Skip   3

Turns
- Front   3
- Rear   3

Ballhandling

Passing and catching
- Bean bag drills   K
- Large ball drills   K
- Fleece ball drills   K
- Pass and catch drills   1
- Pass and catch drills with partner   2-3
- Baseball pass   3

Ball and body moves   3

Dribbling
- Bounce to self   K
- Bounce and move   1
- Low control/power   2
- Around obstacles   3

Shooting

Lay-ups
- Strong hand   3

Set shots   3

Rebounding

Capture and chin

Defending

On the ball
- Stance   2-3
- Zigzag   2-3
- Ball-you-basket   2-3

Off the ball
- Stance   2-3

Fundamentals Table (Grades 4-6)

Footwork

Stance, starts, stops and steps
- Offensive triple threat   4-6
    - → Direct drive   4-6
    - → Crossover   4-6
- Defensive stance and steps
    - → On ball   4
    - → Off ball   4-6
    - → Post defense   4-6
- V-cut   4-6
- 180 degree change   4-6
- Quick stop   4-6
- Stride stop   4-6

Turns
- Front   4
- Rear   5
- Front and rear   6

Jumping
- One foot   4
- Two foot   4

Ballhandling

Passing and catching
- One hand push/flick   5-6
- Two-hand chest   4-6
- Two-hand overhead   5-6
- Baseball   6
- Two-hand catching   4-6

Ball and body drills   4-6

Dribbling
- Low control/power   4-6
- Speed   4-6
- Changes
    - → Crossover   4-6
    - → Pullback crossover   6

Shooting

Lay-ups
- Right and left hand   4-6
- Progression   4-6
- Power   4-6

Set/jump shots
- Progression   4-6
- Set shots   4-6
- Jump shots   6

Free throw shot   4-6

Rebounding

Two hand, two feet, chin   4-6

Defensive
- Blockouts   5-6

Defending

On the ball
- Live ball   4-6
- Dribbler   4-6
- Dead ball   6

Off the ball
- Stances   4-6
- Post defense   4-6

Off the ball to on the ball
- Closeouts   5-6

Jump to ball and basket   6

Team Strategies

Pass and cut   4-6

Catch, face, basket, and drive   4-6

Fundamentals Table (Grades 7-8)

Footwork

Stance, starts, stops, and steps
- Offensive triple threat   7-8
- Defensive stance and steps 7-8

Starting
- Direct drive   7-8
- Crossover   7-8
- Rocker drive   7-8
- Lift and drive   7-8

Stepping
- Running
  - → Change of pace   7-8
  - → Stutter   8
- V-cut   7-8
- 180 degree change   7-8

Turning   7

Stopping
- Quick stop   7-8
- Stride stop   7-8
- Triple stop   8

Ballhandling

Passing
- One-hand push/flick   7-8
- One-hand push/flick bounce   7-8
- Two-hand chest   7-8
- Two-hand chest bounce   7-8

Catching   7

Dribbling
- Low control/power   7-8
- Speed   7-8
- Changes
  - → Crossover   7-8
  - → Pullback crossover   7-8
  - → Head and shoulders   7-8

Shooting

Lay-ups
- Right and left hand   7
- Power   7-8

Three-point shot
- Footwork   8

Set/jump shots
- Progression   7-8
- Bank   8
- Competitive   8

Free throw shot
- Grooving the shot   7-8
- Competition   8

Rebounding

Offensive   8

Defensive   8

Defending

Stance
- On the ball
  - → Live ball   7-8
  - → Dribbler   7-8
  - → Dead ball   7-8
- Off ball
  - → Closed/denial stance   7-8
  - → Open/pistols stance   7-8
  - → Post stance   7-8
- Off the ball to on the ball
  - → Closeouts   7-8
- Jump to ball and basket   7-8

Defending screens
- Over   8
- Under   8
- Hedge and help   8

Fundamentals Table (Grades 7-8) continued

Setting and Using Screens

Off ball
- Screener   7-8
- Cuts
  - ➜ Pop/fill   7-8
  - ➜ Curl   8
- Screener
  - ➜ Pop/fill-flare   7-8
  - ➜ Curl-fill   8

Post Moves

Positioning   7-8

Receiving   7-8

Scoring moves
- Face/jump shot   7-8
- Power   7-8

Team Strategies

Fast break
- 2-on-1   7-8
- 3-on-2   8

Zone offense
- Perimeter
  - ➜ Reversals   7-8
  - ➜ Turnbacks   7-8
  - ➜ Dribble down   8
- Post
  - ➜ Partner post moves   7-8

Fundamentals Table (Grades 9-10)

Footwork

Stance, starts, stops, and steps
- Offensive triple threat
- Defensive stance and steps

Starting
- Direct drive
- Crossover
- Rocker drive
- Lift and drive

Stepping
- Running
  - → Change of pace
  - → Stutter
- V-cut
- 180 degree change

Turning

Stopping
- Quick stop
- Stride stop
- Triple stop

Ballhandling

Passing
- One-hand push/flick
- One-hand push/flick bounce
- Two-hand chest
- Two-hand chest bounce
- Spin bounce   9-10

Catching

Dribbling
- Low control/power
- Speed
- Changes
  - → Crossover
  - → Pullback crossover

- → Head and shoulders
- → Head and shoulders
  crossover   9-10
- → Spin/whirl   9-10
- → Rocker   10

Shooting

Lay-ups
- Right and left hand
- Power
- Reverse   9
- Hook   9-10

Three-point shot
- Footwork
- From pass
  - → Skip   9-10
  - → Penetration   9-10
- From dribble
  - → Drives   9-10

Set/jump shots
- Progression
- Bank
- Competitive

Free throw shot
- Grooving the shot
- Competition

Rebounding

Offensive

Defensive

Fundamentals Table (Grades 9-10) continued

Defending

Stance
- On the ball
  - → Live ball
  - → Dribbler
  - → Dead ball
- Off ball
  - → Closed/denial stance
  - → Open/pistols stance
  - → Post stance
- Off the ball to on the ball
  - → Closeouts
- Jump to ball and basket

Defending screens
- Over
- Under
- Hedge and help
- Switch   9-10
- Trap   9-10

Setting and Using Screens

On ball
- Defense not switch   9-10
- Defense Switch   9-10

Off ball
- Screener
- Cuts
  - → Pop/fill
  - → Curl
  - → Flare   9-10
  - → Back   10
- Screener
  - → Pop/fill-flare
  - → Curl-fill
  - → Flare-fill   9-10
  - → Back-fill   10

Post Moves

Positioning

Receiving

Scoring moves
- Face/jump shot
- Power
- Jump hook   9-10

Team Strategies

Fast break
- 2-on-1
- 3-on-2

Zone offense
- Perimeter
  - → Reversals
  - → Turnbacks
  - → Dribble down
  - → Push   9-10
  - → Loop   10
- Post
  - → Partner post moves
  - → Drive reaction   9-10

Fundamentals Table (Grades 11-12)

Footwork

Stance, starts, stops, and steps
- Offensive triple threat
- Defensive stance and steps

Starting
- Direct drive
- Crossover
- Rocker drive
- Lift and drive

Stepping
- Running
  → Change of pace
  → Stutter
- V-cut
- 180 degree change

Turning

Stopping
- Quick stop
- Stride stop
- Triple stop

Ballhandling

Passing
- One-hand push/flick
- One-hand push/flick bounce
- Two-hand chest
- Two-hand chest bounce
- Spin bounce

Catching

Dribbling
- Low control/power
- Speed
- Changes
  → Crossover
  → Pullback crossover

→ Head and shoulders
→ Head and shoulders crossover
→ Spin/whirl
→ Rocker

Shooting

Lay-ups
- Right and left hand
- Power
- Reverse
- Hook
- Running one-hander   11-12

Three-point shot
- Footwork
- From pass
  → Skip
  → Penetration
  → Fast break   11-12
  → Screens   11-12
- From dribble
  → Drives
  → Fast Break   11-12
  → Screens

Set/jump shots
- Progression
- Bank
- Competitive

Free throw shot

Rebounding

Offensive

Defensive

Fundamentals Table (Grades 11-12) continued

Defending

Stance
- On the ball
  - → Live ball
  - → Dribbler
  - → Dead ball
- Off ball
  - → Closed/denial stance
  - → Open/pistols stance
  - → Post stance
- Off ball to on ball
  - → Closeouts
- Jump to ball and basket

Defending screens
- Over
- Under
- Hedge and help
- Switch
- Trap

Setting and Using Screens

On ball
- Defense not switch
- Defense Switch
- Step back outside   11-12

Off ball
- Screener
- Cuts
  - → Pop/fill
  - → Curl
  - → Flare
  - → Back
- Screener
  - → Pop/fill-flare
  - → Curl-fill
  - → Flare-fill
  - → Back-fill

Post Moves

Positioning

Receiving

Scoring moves
- Face/jump shot
- Power
- Jump hook

Team Strategies

Fast break
- 2-on-1
- 3-on-2

Zone offense
- Perimeter
  - → Reversals
  - → Turnbacks
  - → Dribble down
  - → Push
  - → Loop
- Post
  - → Partner post moves
  - → Drive reaction
  - → Stepouts   11-12
  - → Slips   11-12

REFERENCES

American Sport Education Program. (2001). *Coaching Youth Basketball*. Champaign, IL: Human Kinetics.

Burnett, Darrell J. (2001). *Youth Sports and Self-Esteem: A Guide for Parents*. Spalding Sports Library.

Dickinson, A. and Garchow, K. (eds.). (1992). *Youth Basketball: A Complete Handbook*. Dubuque, IA: Brown & Benchmark.

Drake, B. M. (1997). "Is winning the only thing [microform]: Goal orientations and team norms, predictions of legitimacy, rating of intentionally injurious sport acts" thesis (M.S.). Purdue University.

Drennan, M.L. (1994). "Incentive motivation of female basketball players across three age levels" [microform] thesis (M.S.). Springfield College.

Faucher, D. (2000). *The Baffled Parent's Guide to Coaching Youth Basketball*. Camden, ME: Ragged Mountain Press.

Grawer, R. (2003). *Youth Basketball Skills and Drills* 2nd ed. Monterey, CA: Coaches Choice.

Hutchinson, J. (1989). *Coaching Girls' Basketball Successfully*. Champaign, IL: Leisure Press.

Kozub, F.M. (May/June 2001). "Using task cards to help beginner basketball players self-assess." *Strategies* 14 (5), 18-22.

Martens, R, and V Seedeldt (Eds.). (1979). *Guidelines for Children's Sports*, AAHPERD.

Martens, R. (1997). *Successful Coaching* 2nd ed. Champaign, IL: Human Kinetics.

McCarthy, J. P. (1996). *Youth Basketball: The Guide for Coaches & Parents*. Cincinnati, OH: Betterway Books.

McKay, L. L. (1997). "Biomechanical parameters influencing fourth grade children's free throw shooting" [microform] thesis (M. Ed.). Temple University.

Paye, B. (2001). *Youth Basketball Drills*. Champaign, IL: Human Kinetics.

Pendleton, S. (2001). "Motivating Female Athletes for Success in Basketball." *Coach and Athletic Director* 70 (7), 96-7.

Poisson, C. F. (1999). "A qualitative investigation of the contact theory/hypothesis and a middle school boys' basketball team" [microform] thesis (D.P.E.). Springfield College.

Rukavina, Paul Bernard. (1998). "A coach's intervention to enhance practice, motor time, and skill in youth basketball players" [microform] thesis (M.S.). Arizona State University.

Sigman, D. (2000). "Stop Getting Beat Backdoor!" *Coach and Athletic Director* 70 (2), 46-8.

Smith, J.W. (1997). "The effect of an intervention program on cohesion with ninth grade female basketball teams" [microform] thesis (M.S.). Oregon State University.

Smoll, Frank L., Magill, Richard A., and Ash, Michael J. (1988). *Children in Sport* 3rd ed. Champaign, IL: Human Kinetics.

Starr, M.T. (1990). "The relationship of conflict styles and team cohesion of high school basketball players" [microform] thesis (M.A.). Kent State University.

Weeks, D.L. and Kordus, R.N. (1998). "Relative frequency of knowledge of performance and motor skill learning." *Research Quarterly for Exercise and Sport* 69 (3), 224-30.

Wolff, Rick. (1998). *Good Sports*. Champaign, IL: Sports Publishing, Inc.

ADDITIONAL RESOURCES

Coaching Youth Sports
An electronic newsletter for coaches, athletes, and parents that presents information about learning and performing sport skills. (courseware.vt.edu/users/rstratto/CYS/)

The Institute for the Study of Youth Sports
This institute at Michigan State University researches the benefits and detriments of participation in youth sports; produces educational materials for parents, coaches, officials, and administrators; and provides educational programs for coaches, officials, administrators, and parents. (ed-web3.educ.msu.edu/ysi/)

Kids' Sports Bulletin Board
Youth sports site offering advice and information for coaches, parents, and kids. Provides monthly player and coach recognition and prizes. (www.coachjerry.com)

National Alliance for Youth Sports
Nonprofit association that seeks to improve the current state of youth sports. Web site includes information on education, development, activities, and links. (www.nays.org)

National Youth Sports Safety Foundation
National nonprofit, educational organization that focuses on injury prevention, emergency plans, individual risk factors, and coaching education. (www.nyssf.org)

North American Youth Sport Institute
In-service training and technical support for parents and leaders in youth sport, recreation, physical education, fitness, and health. (www.naysi.com)

OurTeam.com
Collection of links to youth basketball and high school teams, mainly in the United States. (www.ourteam.com)

Teamanizer Coaching Software
Designed for youth basketball and other sports, this program helps with scheduling, statistics, and creating game plans. (www.teamanizer.com)

Youth-Sports.com
This web site has free articles, a free newsletter, coaching tools, and instructional products that help parents, coaches, and children involved in youth sports. The site also sponsors a coloring contest for children. (www.youth-sports.com)

YouthSports USA
Users can develop and maintain community web pages for youth sports teams, read tips and articles, or search for specific leagues by state. (www.ysusa.com)

ABOUT THE AUTHORS

Jerry Krause is the director of basketball operations for Gonzaga University (the Zags) in Spokane, Washington. He has coached and taught basketball at all levels for over 40 years. The author of 13 books on coaching basketball and over 30 instructional videos, Krause is the chairman of the NABC Research Committee and former chairman of the NCAA Basketball Rules Committee.

In 1998, Krause received the prestigious NABC Cliff Wells Appreciation Award for his lifetime contributions to basketball. He was inducted into the NAIA Basketball Hall of Fame in March 2002. He is a member of the National Association for Sports and Physical Education and is in their hall of fame as both a coach and a physical educator.

Curtis Janz is in his 13th season as head assistant coach at Oklahoma Christian University (OCU). Janz played at OCU and earned a masters degree at the University of Central Oklahoma. He and Dan Hays share a strong coaching relationship that has developed the OCU basketball program into one of the finest NAIA programs in the nation.

Janz is an associate professor of physical education and assistant director of the OCU "Cage Camps," one of the largest and most successful basketball camps in the country. It attracts athletes from all 50 states, as well as 12 foreign countries. This is his first basketball coaching book.

James H. Conn is a professor in the department of health and human performance at Central Missouri State University. Conn has 34 years experience in teaching and coaching, and 10 years experience as a department chair in higher education. He currently teaches courses in legal issues, risk management, sport facility management, sport marketing, and motor learning. In 2002, the Missouri AAHPERD selected him as their "Scholar of the Year."

Conn has published two books, written three book chapters, and published numerous articles in the JLASPE, JOHPERD, Strategies, and the Physical Educators. He is a frequent presenter at state, regional, national, and international organizations. Conn has consulted on numerous court proceedings. He has a B.A. from the University of Northern Colorado, an M.S. from Eastern Washington University, and a Ph.D. from Southern Illinois University.